FACTS ON FILE

Environment
atlas

David R. Wright

 Facts On File, Inc.

Contents

NOTE: Each continent is color coded on THIS contents page
AND on the map opposite AND on the heading of each page.

FRONT COVER PHOTO ACKNOWLEDGMENTS:
BIOFOTOS IJ. M. Pearson bottom
Soames Summerhays top right
Tony Stone Images /Paul Berger top left
Rupert Everts bottom left
Roger Mear center   [*For further credits to photographs see page 96.*]

WWF–UK Advisor *Alison Manners*
Picture Research *Lisa MacGregor*
Concept *Steven Wright*

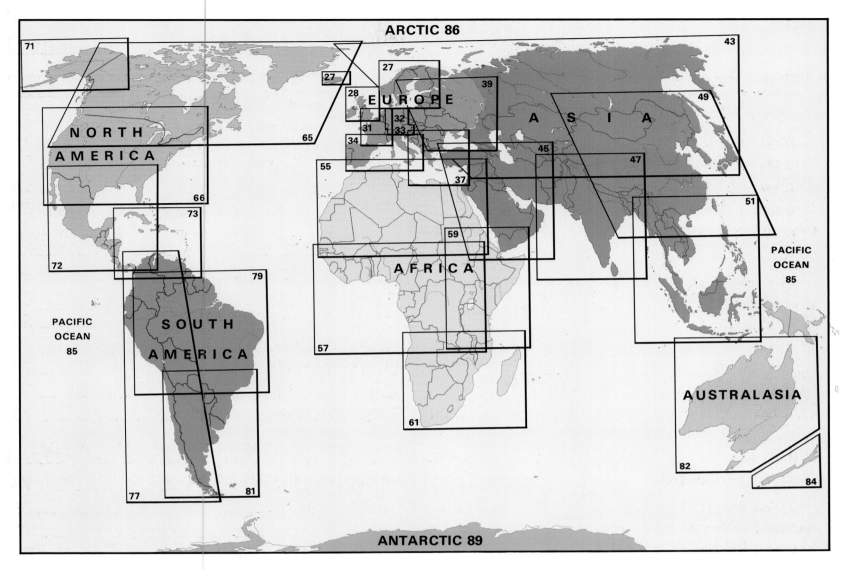

Text © 1992, 1997 David R. Wright
Maps © 1992, 1997 George Philip Limited

Cartography by Philip's

First published in Great Britain in 1992 by
George Philip Limited,
in association with the World Wide Fund for Nature
(WWF–UK)*
Revised edition 1997

First published in the United States of America by
Facts On File, Inc.

Facts On File, Inc.
11 Penn Plaza
New York, NY10001

Facts On File books are available at special discounts
when purchased in bulk quantities for businesses,
associations, institutions or sales promotions.

Please call our Special Sales Department in New York
at (212) 967–8800 or (800) 322–8755.

You can find Facts On File on the World Wide Web
at http://www.factsonfile.com

**Library of Congress Cataloging-in-Publication
Data available**

ISBN 0–8160–3715–9

Printed in China

10 9 8 7 6 5 4 3 2 1

* Note: In the United States, WWF refers to the
World Wildlife Fund.

Introducing maps

▶ **Latitude.** *Every map in this atlas shows the numbers of the lines of latitude at the sides. The globe here shows the Equator at zero degrees and the tropics between 23½ degrees north and 23½ degrees south of the Equator. Except in high mountains it is never cold in the tropics. There is no "winter" or "summer," but there may be a "wet season" and a "dry season." The coldest lands are between 66½° and 90°. It's hardly ever hot there.*

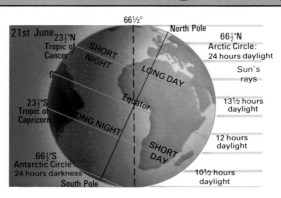

◀ **Day and night.** *Did you know that every place on Earth has a total of half its year in daylight and half in darkness? The Equator has 12 hours of daylight (6 a.m. to 6 p.m.) and 12 hours of darkness each day. The further you go away from the tropics, the longer the summer days become and the shorter the winter days. This is why northern Norway is "the land of the midnight sun" in summer (June) — but is "the land of midday night" in winter.*

◀ **Longitude.** *Lines of longitude all go from the North Pole southward to the South Pole — rather like the segments of a peeled orange. On this postage stamp, 0° (the Greenwich Meridian) is shown on a satellite photograph of the world. It "runs" from the North Pole through London, France and Spain to the Sahara Desert, West Africa, and the South Pole. Longitude tells you how far west or east you are from 0°. Fiji, in the Pacific, is at 180°.*

▶ **Altitude.** *A black triangle is the symbol for the top of a mountain — with its height, or altitude, in feet. If a mountain is high enough it can have snow on it, even at the Equator! (See diagram of Mt Kilimanjaro on page 53.) The atlas maps show height clearly. The "shadows" give an impression of steep slopes, and the colors explain the height. We use shades of green for lowland and brown for highland. Very high land is violet, and the highest land of all is white.*

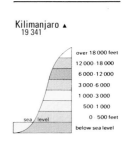

THE KEY TO THE MAPS

Blue is for water – rivers, lakes and seas. We use *italic* (sloping) letters for naming rivers, lakes and seas.

Red circles and squares show big towns and cities. We haven't put all of them on some of the maps because it would make them too crowded.

Underlining shows the capital city of a country. That is where the government meets, and where important decisions are made about most environmental matters.

Scale. A map at a scale of "1:40 000 000" means that the real distance on the ground is 40 *million* times bigger than it is on the map. One inch represents 40 million inches – therefore one inch represents 640 miles.

The green area on the little (inset) map shows where the region is in the world.

[The letters across the top of the map and the numbers down the side of the map are there to help you find a place you look up in the Index (pages 92–95). Manila, for example, is indexed as 51 D2 – "square" D2 on page 51.]

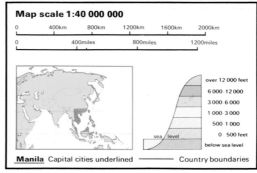

THE COUNTRIES OF THE WORLD

are shown clearly on a map at the start of each continent. And the boundaries of the countries are shown by a red line on the area maps. These boundaries are very important, but the actions of people and government in one country can affect other countries.

A government that *cares* can:
- *Create* National Parks
- *Safeguard* endangered species
- *Help* soil conservation
- *Stop* forests being destroyed
- *Plant* some new forests

VEGETATION. Each continent starts with a vegetation map. In many places, people have removed much of the natural vegetation – but it's still worth knowing what was there – and what would return if people let it do so. The natural vegetation is perfectly suited to the climate, and it follows a logical pattern based on temperature and rainfall. For example, most palm trees can't survive frost – so most grow in hot countries. And the pine trees of Russia wouldn't thrive in the hot, wet tropics.

Introducing environment

It is helpful to think of *three* major environments in our world. The three types of landscape could be called "Wildscape," "Farmscape" and "Townscape." These words aren't in the dictionary yet – but they should be, because they are a useful key to understanding our world. Of course, the boundaries are difficult to define, and they are always changing, but it's a good start....

> **"WILDSCAPES"**… are where nature still dominates.
>
> **"FARMSCAPES"**… are where people, animals and crops share the land and the environment.
>
> **"TOWNSCAPES"**… are where people dominate.

◄ **"WILDSCAPES"** are areas where nature has not been destroyed by people – yet. Wildscapes can be forest or grassland, desert or savanna, mountain or tundra, and the world was once all "wildscape." This elephant and baby are walking through grassland in Africa, with thick palm trees near a hidden river in the background. Wildscapes are best for animals, birds and plants, but they are becoming smaller and fewer every year because farmland and towns are spreading. And the number of wild animals is far fewer than it used to be.

► **"FARMSCAPES"** can be quite good for nature and for wildlife. In this view of countryside in Hampshire, England, birds and insects can live and move in the trees and the hedgerows – and even feast on the ripe corn. But if the hedges are cut down and poisonous sprays are used on the crops, farmland can almost become a "wildlife desert." Farmscapes vary widely with the climate and the type of agriculture. They could be this lovely scene, or the wheatlands of the Canadian prairies, or the cattle ranches of Argentina, or the rice paddies of South and Southeast Asia.

◄ **"TOWNSCAPES"** are usually the least good place for wildlife – but even here there is room for nature too. This stork has built a superb nest on a chimney pot – and two babies have hatched. And yet there is not a blade of grass and not a plant or flower or twig in sight. The storks found the twigs for their nest in the town park. Some towns and cities have big open areas that are carefully managed – such as Hampstead Heath in London or the Bois de Boulogne in Paris. And although towns are spreading fast in almost all parts of the world, built-up areas still take up less than one-hundredth of the world's land surface.

"GREENING" THE CITY

In the suburbs of our towns and cities, there is more room for plants, bushes and trees – and for birdlife too. If you live in a suburb, why not plant some plants and bushes from other parts of the world? (See page 49.) In suburban gardens, or in school grounds, you can get pieces of wildscape, where wild plants are allowed to grow. But more "suburban sprawl" can mean less farmscape and wildscape: it's a real problem for planners.

The world's land

THE WORLD'S BIGGEST DESERTS

Desert	Location	Area in sq miles*
Sahara	North Africa	3,200,000
Australian	Australia	600,000
Arabian	S.W. Asia	500,000
Gobi	Central Asia	400,000
Kalahari	S.W. Africa	200,000

* But they are getting bigger – see page 14.

THE WORLD'S LONGEST RIVERS

River	Location	Length in miles*
Nile	Africa	4150
Amazon	S. America	4000
Mississippi	N. America	3740
Yenisey	Russia	3450
Yangtze	China	3340

* Measured from the most distant tributary.

▲ *Lulworth Cove, Dorset, UK. This is a peaceful scene now – but look how the rock strata have been bent and folded in the past! The sea has eroded these cliffs, changing the shape of the coastline.*

The map shows five important things:
1. Most of the world's land is in the Northern Hemisphere.
2. Most of Africa and South America are in the "tropics."
3. Very little of the world's land is south of the Tropic of Capricorn.
4. The "Middle East" (Southwest Asia) is the only place on Earth where THREE continents come close together.
5. Asia is HUGE! This map "projection" makes the northern parts of the world bigger than they really are, but even so Asia is the largest continent.

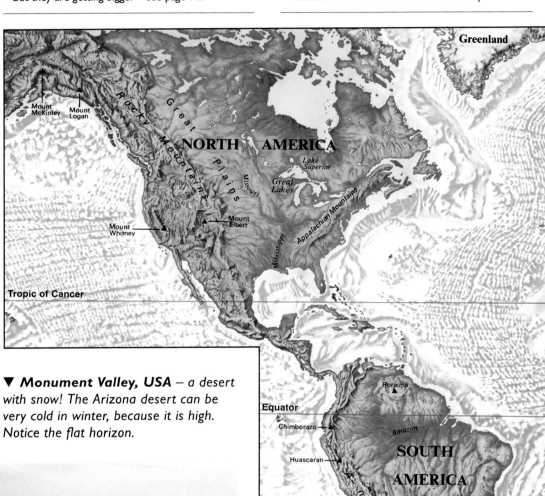

▼ *Monument Valley, USA – a desert with snow! The Arizona desert can be very cold in winter, because it is high. Notice the flat horizon.*

▶ *Which continent is missing? See page 88.*

THE WORLD'S HIGHEST MOUNTAINS

Continent	Highest peak	Height in feet
Asia*	Everest	29,028
S. America	Aconcagua	22,835
N. America	McKinley	20,322
Africa	Kilimanjaro	19,341
E. Europe	Elbrus	18,481
Antarctica	Vinson Massif	16,067
W. Europe	Mont Blanc	15,771
Australasia	Wilhelm	14,791

* All the "top ten" highest mountains are in the Himalayas of Asia, but the Andes is the world's longest mountain range.

MOUNTAINS OF THE WORLD

This drawing exaggerates steepness and "squeezes up" the continents to fit in 30 of the world's highest peaks.

[Mountain heights in feet]

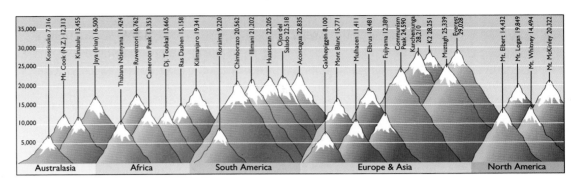

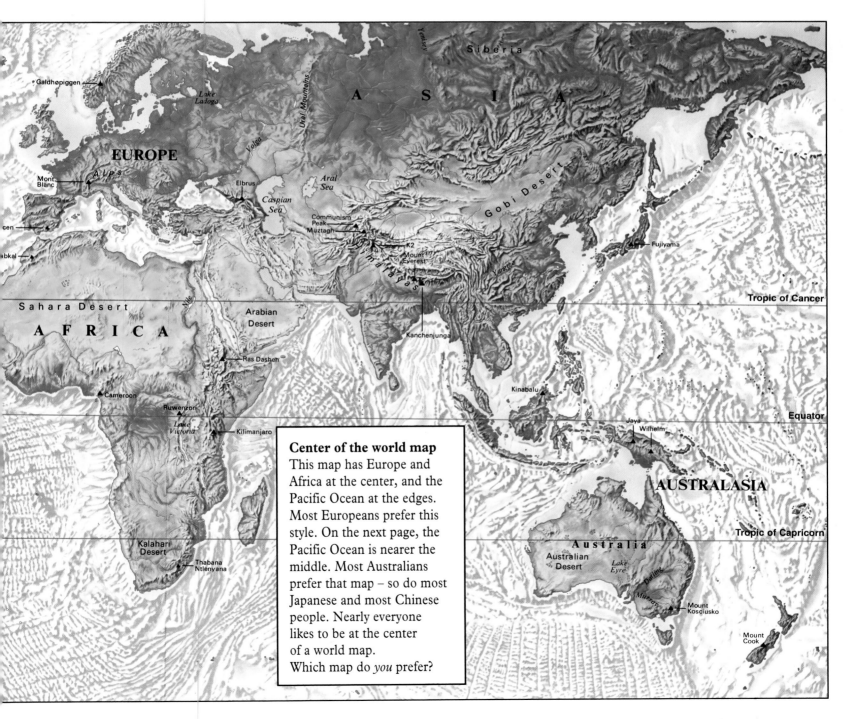

Center of the world map
This map has Europe and Africa at the center, and the Pacific Ocean at the edges. Most Europeans prefer this style. On the next page, the Pacific Ocean is nearer the middle. Most Australians prefer that map – so do most Japanese and most Chinese people. Nearly everyone likes to be at the center of a world map.
Which map do *you* prefer?

The world's oceans

The oceans of the world matter so much to the environment:
• Ocean currents affect the climate – for example, a warm current warms up Northwest Europe, and a cold current cools western South America.
• The oceans have a wonderful variety of seabirds and fish, but overfishing is doing terrible harm to many of these creatures.

• Ocean waves erode parts of the world's land, and build new lands elsewhere.
• The oceans are all linked together: any change can affect faraway places.
• Oceans are where hurricanes, cyclones and typhoons start.
• The oceans' seabeds are rich in minerals that could be useful to industries – but mining could add to pollution problems.

The size of the world's oceans:
Pacific 69,715,000 square miles;
Atlantic 35,841,000 sq miles;
Indian 28,680,000 sq miles;
Arctic 5,467,000 sq miles.

Did you realize? If you could "drop" Mt. Everest into the Mariana Trench, it would vanish completely!

▲ *A humbback whale near Ogasawara Island, Japan. There were once 50 times more whales than there are today.*

POLLUTION OF THE OCEANS
Our oceans are becoming more polluted from three main sources:
1. Millions of tons of **oil** are released into the oceans every year. Some comes from oil tankers that collide or run aground. Some comes from tankers washing out their tanks – although this is illegal.
2. Pollution from **factories** and **sewage** from towns near the coast often goes straight into the sea.
3. **Rivers** carry polluted water from inland towns, factories and farms.
Ocean pollution is now recognized as a major problem. The United Nations Environment Program (UNEP) is trying to get agreement from most countries to reduce pollution.

ATLANTIC OCEAN   **INDIAN**

▶ **The ocean trenches** are deepest in the Pacific – but all the three big oceans have deep trenches: they are clearly marked on the map. Very little life exists there: the majority of sea creatures live near the surface and the light of the sun. Less than one-fiftieth of the oceans are trenches, which are zones of weakness in the Earth's crust. Earthquakes are frequent there, and these can cause "tsunamis" – a Japanese word for a huge wave that can travel hundreds of miles across the Pacific.

DEPTHS OF THE OCEANS

This cross section exaggerates steepness and "squeezes up" the ocean to fit in 15 deep trenches.

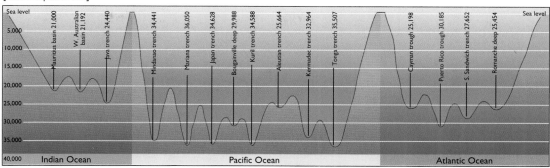

[Ocean depths in feet]

Sea level / 5,000 / 10,000 / 15,000 / 20,000 / 25,000 / 30,000 / 35,000 / 40,000

Mauritius basin 21,000 · W. Australian basin 21,192 · Java trench 24,440 · Mindanao trench 34,441 · Mariana trench 36,050 · Japan trench 34,628 · Bougainville deep 29,988 · Kurii trench 34,588 · Aleutian trench 25,664 · Kermadec trench 32,964 · Tonga trench 35,507 · Cayman trough 25,198 · Puerto Rico trough 30,185 · S. Sandwich trench 27,652 · Romanche deep 25,454

Indian Ocean · Pacific Ocean · Atlantic Ocean

Could these be the two most important pages in the atlas? It is easy to forget that the Earth's surface is seven-tenths ocean, and only three-tenths land, because most atlas maps stop where the ocean starts! This map shows the oceans clearly, as well as ridges on the ocean's floor and deep ocean trenches.

OCEAN

PACIFIC OCEAN

The world's climate

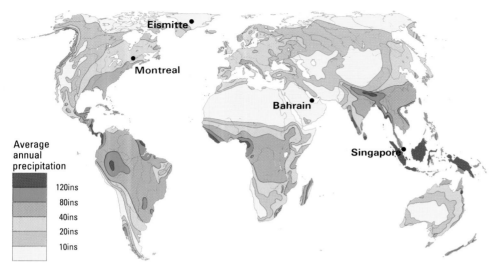

Average annual precipitation
- 120ins
- 80ins
- 40ins
- 20ins
- 10ins

WATER: THE KEY TO LIFE

You could say that the map of world "precipitation" (mostly rain, but also snow and hail) is the most important map for understanding environments. Where there is water, plants can grow – and animals and people can live.

The map shows the average precipitation, but some areas have big changes from year to year. It shows the total for an average year – but it cannot show that some places have a short wet season and a long dry season.

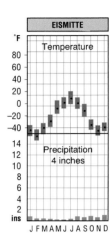

EISMITTE
Temperature
Precipitation 4 inches
J F M A M J J A S O N D

WHERE DOES IT RAIN LEAST?

The map shows all the world's dry areas in yellow – central Asia and the Arctic, for example, get very little rain or snow. In part of northern Chile, no rain fell for 400 years!

The graph shows Bahrain, in the Middle East. This town has a desert climate, with just a few days of rain in the winter. On average, Bahrain has one-seventh as much rain as London, and one-thirtieth as much as Singapore. But the "average" figure hides big changes from year to year in rainfall totals in deserts. Some desert areas are even drier.

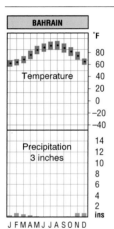

BAHRAIN
Temperature
Precipitation 3 inches
J F M A M J J A S O N D

WHERE DOES IT RAIN MOST?

The world map shows areas of heavy rain in dark blue. Almost all these areas are in the tropics, and the wettest place in the world is in Colombia, South America.

The graph shows that Singapore has heavy rain in all months of the year – usually in heavy storms in the afternoon. It has four times more rain in a year than London or Paris. There are no seasons: it is very humid (hot and sticky) all year, just like the air above a swimming pool. Lots of oil is used for power to provide air-conditioning for shops, offices and hotels.

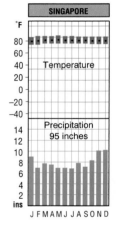

SINGAPORE
Temperature
Precipitation 95 inches
J F M A M J J A S O N D

MONTREAL
Temperature
Precipitation 38 inches
J F M A M J J A S O N D

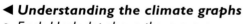

◀ Understanding the climate graphs
- *Each black dot shows the average temperature for a month.*
- *The top of the red line shows the average maximum (highest) temperature.*
- *The bottom of the red line shows the average minimum (lowest) temperature.*
- *The blue blocks show the average precipitation (rain, snow, hail) for each month.*
- *The figures at the side mark the temperature in degrees Fahrenheit and the precipitation in inches.*
- *The letters at the bottom are the initials of the months of the year.*

ISN'T IT STRANGE? Water is "H_2O": it is made of hydrogen and oxygen. There's lots of hydrogen and oxygen in the air, yet we still haven't found a cheap and easy way of making water!

▲ Can we see climate?
Yes, we can! Here an afternoon thunderstorm is about to burst over the Amazon rain forest in Brazil. Even the forest is flooded! There are no seasons here: it is always hot and wet. The climate graph would look similar to the one for Singapore (above).

THE WORLD IN JANUARY ▶

Just look at how cold it gets in northern Asia and Canada in January! Animals and plants in these areas adapt to survive the bitter cold. Northwestern Europe is fortunate: it is much less cold than other northern areas, because of a warm ocean current called the North Atlantic Drift. In January, the sun is directly overhead near the Tropic of Capricorn, at 23½° south of the Equator. The hottest places in January are the deserts of Australia.

◀ *Eismitte, on the Greenland ice sheet, has an amazing climate! The average temperature is colder than −40 degrees Fahrenheit in February and it is 5 degrees Fahrenheit even in July! Yet it has as little precipitation as the Sahara Desert! Eismitte means "middle of the ice sheet."*

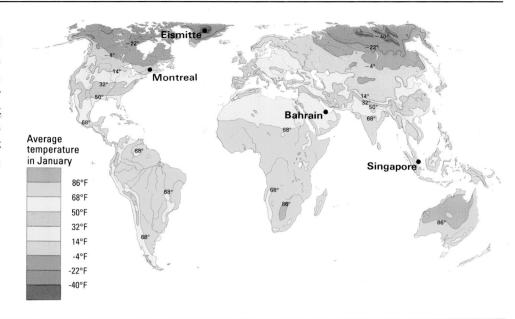

Average temperature in January

86°F
68°F
50°F
32°F
14°F
-4°F
-22°F
-40°F

THE WORLD IN JULY ▶

In July, the sun is directly overhead near the Tropic of Cancer, at 23½° north of the Equator. All the cold green shading has vanished from the map. Nowhere in the world is really cold in July, except for central Greenland and Antarctica. It is winter in the Southern Hemisphere – but it is much less cold than in the north in January.

There is much more orange shading on the July map than on the January map. Orange shows an average temperature of over 86°F, so daytime figures will be much higher. Plan your visit to the Sahara in January, and to the Australian Desert in July!

The places that are yellow or brown on *both* maps are the only parts of the world that are hot all year.

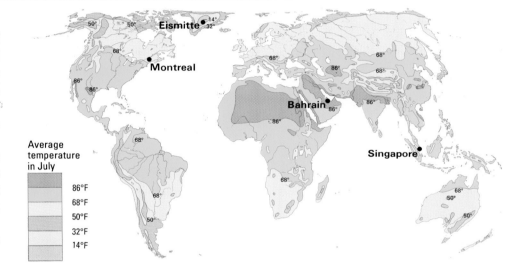

Average temperature in July

86°F
68°F
50°F
32°F
14°F

PALMS: TREES THAT LOVE THE HEAT

Some palm trees need a hot, wet climate. Others, such as the one on this coin from the Gambia, in West Africa, don't mind a dry season. And date palms (left) actually prefer a dry climate as long as their deep roots can reach water. Palms hate frost, and are clear evidence of an area with a warm climate all year round.

▶ *PUZZLE PICTURE . . .*
These strange objects are not lumps of sugar! But what are they? And where? And why? And how?
(Answers on page 96.)

▲ *Can we see climate?*
Yes, we can! This arctic fox is at Churchill, beside Hudson Bay in Canada, in November. It is bitterly cold. This view is completely different in summer: the snow disappears, and the fox will not have the white fur that acts as camouflage in winter.

Fragile Earth

The Earth's crust is between 3 miles and 25 miles thick. The crust is thickest under the continents, and thinnest under the oceans. The map shows how it is divided into "plates" – rather like the cracked shell of a hard-boiled egg.

Where two plates are pushing together, earthquakes and volcanoes are likely. For example, the Pacific Plate is being forced down under North America at the rate of a few tenths of an inch every year. So people in parts of California expect earthquakes, and buildings need to be specially strong.

Whenever there is an earthquake in the news, try checking this map to see which two plates are colliding. The very day that this page was written, there was an earthquake in Costa Rica, Central America.

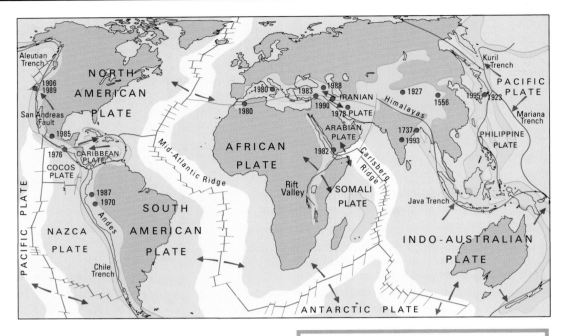

	Stable land area
	Sea
	Zones of sea-floor spreading
	Main earthquake areas
● 1988	Major earthquakes with dates
✕ ✕ ✕	Plate boundaries
←	Direction of plate movements

▼ *Earthquake in Mexico.* *The "Cruz Roja" workers are carrying an injured person on a stretcher.* The person was inside a modern concrete building, which collapsed after a violent earthquake in 1985. You can see the iron "reinforcements" of the concrete in the foreground – but they were not strong enough. It is possible to build safer buildings, but it is very expensive. Water supply and drains may also be damaged in a big earthquake, so there are health problems as well. Damage is usually worst in cities. Most earthquakes happen in countries that border the Pacific Ocean, for example Japan in 1995.*

* "Cruz Roja" is Spanish for "Red Cross."

THE RICHTER SCALE is used to measure the power of earthquakes. The bigger the number, the bigger the "quake." Each number has 10 times as much energy released as the number before – so Scale 7 is a million times more powerful than Scale 1.

1. People not aware of the small shocks.
2. Seismograph printout "wobbles."
3. Movement can be felt by people.
4. Light tremors; slight damage.
5. Some buildings damaged.
6. Shaking: some buildings collapse.
7. Many buildings destroyed.
8. Ground "shakes"; huge cracks.
9. Massive destruction . . . .

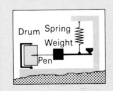

◀ **A seismograph** measures force of earthquakes, but how does it work? (Answer on page 96.)

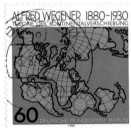

▲ **Continental "drift."** Alfred Wegener developed the idea of the continents moving apart in 1915. The German stamp shows his map of the world millions of years ago. Can you name the continents?*

▼ **Wegener's map** gave us one clue why some animals in Africa are similar to animals in Australia. Which flightless bird lives in which continent?* (*Answers on page 96.)

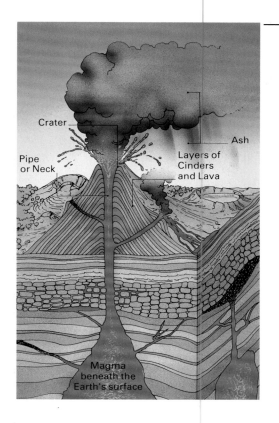

Crater

Ash

Pipe or Neck

Layers of Cinders and Lava

Magma beneath the Earth's surface

FAMOUS VOLCANIC ERUPTIONS

Year	Volcano	Deaths
79	Vesuvius, Pompeii, Italy	16,000
1669	Etna, Sicily, Italy	20,000
1792	Unzen-Dake, Japan	15,000
1815	Tamboro, Java, Indonesia	12,000
1883	Krakatau, Indonesia	50,000
1902	Pelée, Martinique, W. Indies	40,000
1951	Lamington, Papua New Guinea	6000
1966	Kelud, Java, Indonesia	1000
1980	St. Helens, Washington, USA	100
1985	Nevado del Ruiz, Colombia	22,940
1986	Wum, Cameroon	1700
1991	Pinatubo, Philippines	300
1993	Mayon, Philippines	77
1994	Merapi, Indonesia	41

◄ **How a volcano works.** *Magma (molten rock) comes up from far below, and layers of ash and lava make the typical cone shape of a volcano. If the "neck" becomes blocked by solidified lava, a secondary cone may be formed – you can see an active one on the right, and a dormant ("sleeping") one on the left. The main neck of this volcano has been cleared by a big explosion. In the background is a crater lake – caused by an enormous explosion that blew the top off a volcano. Some of the ash will be blown by the wind, and may fall to the ground hundreds of miles away.*

▲ **A helpful sign?** *Lava from a volcano in Hawaii had blocked the road a quarter of a mile away – so a sign was put up to warn motorists. But the volcano kept working and the lava kept flowing. Soon the road had vanished here too.*

▼ **An active volcano in Hawaii.** *This is a "time exposure" photograph. Red-hot cinders from the volcano make red stripes. Some of the lava goes into the sea, and huge clouds of steam rise high into the air. The fertile islands of Hawaii are almost entirely made of cooled lava (see page 71).*

▼ **When "plates" collide.** *The diagram below shows what happens when two plates of the Earth's crust push against each other. The heavier ocean plate is forced down under the lighter continental plate. It does not move smoothly: sometimes there will be a big earthquake shock, shown by the "wobbly" upward arrows. High fold mountains like the Andes and the Himalayas were created by these movements, and many of the world's volcanoes are found at or near plate boundaries. Indonesia has 77 active volcanoes! Volcanoes can also occur where two plates are moving apart – for example in Iceland. There are no big earthquakes in these areas. The volcanoes of Hawaii (see photograph, right) are not on a plate boundary – the crust is much thinner than usual there, and faults allow lava to escape.*

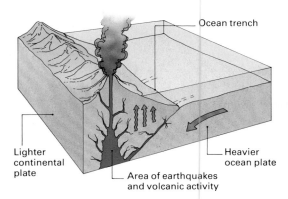

Ocean trench

Lighter continental plate

Heavier ocean plate

Area of earthquakes and volcanic activity

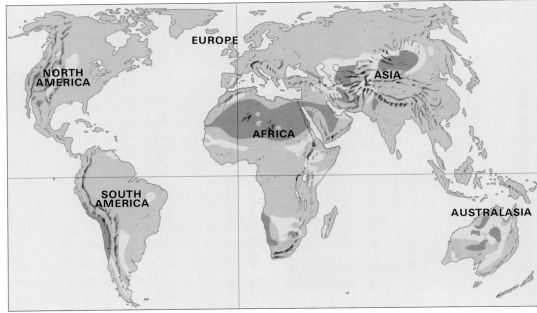

"Desertification" is the word used to describe the spread of deserts. Areas near deserts may become more arid for many reasons: dry winds blowing from the desert; and/or less rainfall; and/or overgrazing; and/or people pumping up too much water.

◀ *A dried-up lake in Australia. The map shows that large parts of Australia are at risk from desertification. Many semiarid areas of the world get good rain in some years, but hardly any rain in other years.*

▲ EXPANDING DESERTS

Existing deserts. These are the areas with very low rainfall; compare with the map on page 10.

High risk of desertification.

Moderate risk of desertification.

Mountainous areas. These have the steepest slopes, and are most liable to gully erosion.

The remaining land areas include high and medium rainfall areas and the vast belts of "tundra" in the Northern Hemisphere. These are marshy in summer, despite the low rainfall.

▼ **Overgrazing** destroyed the grass and bushes, then heavy rainstorms on dry land resulted in water carving these steep gullies in Niger, West Africa. Soil erosion is a huge problem for poor countries; and once it starts, it's very hard to stop.

GULLY EROSION...

is a huge problem in many parts of the "developing" world – once the soil has gone, it cannot be brought back. The hills shown on the stamps were plowed along the contours, to stop gullies forming. The whole landscape really did look like a contour map! It made a big difference: Rwanda had very little erosion, despite steep hills.

▶ **"Let's fight against erosion"** is the slogan (in French) on these stamps from Rwanda. BUT in the terrible civil war of 1994, the environment was severely damaged because the people could not look after the anti-erosion schemes.

▶ DISAPPEARING RAIN FOREST

■ Existing rain forest

■ Former areas of rain forest

▶ **The rain forests** are getting smaller every year, and despite the dangers of "deforestation" they are still being cut down at an alarming rate. There are rain forests in all the continents except Europe and Antarctica – although the biggest forest in the world is in Russia and its neighbors.

▼ **"Environment friendlier"**: a label from our home. We use recycled paper if we can, to help conserve the world's forests. You and your friends can help the world, too.

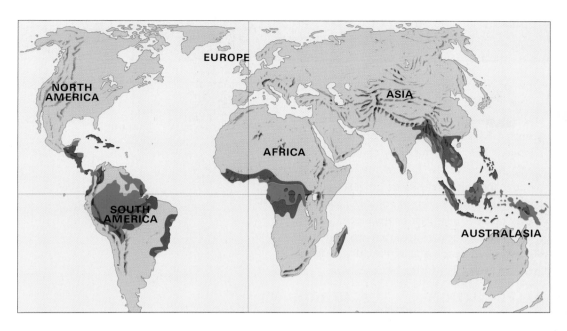

K I T C H E N
T O W E L S

from 100% Recycled Paper

2 ROLLS – 70 SHEETS PER ROLL

▶ **A forest fire at night.** Some forest fires are caused by lightning – for example, when a violent thunderstorm ends a long dry season. Other fires are caused by people – by carelessness, or by vandalism, or to clear land for farming. Either way, it is a great danger to the habitat and its teeming wildlife.

▲ **White pelicans** and their young, Danube delta, Romania. But will their home be kept safe from development?

WETLANDS OF THE WORLD...

are under threat. Wetlands are specially important for birds and other wildlife. There are many types of wetland, including marshes near rivers and deltas of rivers (left), mangrove swamps on tropical coasts (right), and peat bogs on moors. The main threats to wetlands are:
- Pumping out water for towns.
- Draining for farmland – good for people and food, but bad for wildlife.
- Draining for afforestation.
- Draining for tourism at the coast.
- Digging out peat for use in farming – or even for fuel.
- Cutting down mangroves in swamplands for woodchips.

▶ ▼ **Mangrove swamp,** The Gambia, West Africa. The closeup shows a dozen roots from just one plant: there must be millions in the main picture! Mangroves stop erosion and are good habitats for fish and insects.

Planet in danger: 2

One of the main causes of air pollution is the burning of "fossil fuels" – coal, oil and gas – in power stations, factories and homes. Poisonous oxides of sulfur and nitrogen are produced by burning fossil fuels. Acid rain is caused by the sulfur oxides and nitrous oxides in polluted air combining with water vapor and falling as precipitation – acid rain or even acid snow.

The main effects of acid rain are that trees die and lakes become acid, resulting in fewer fish – so fewer fish-eating birds survive.

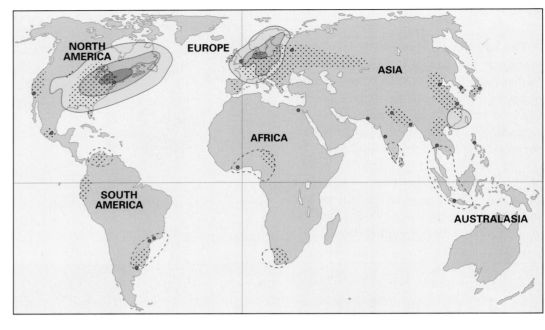

AIR POLLUTION

Main areas with polluted air

Big cities with polluted air

ACID RAIN

Very acid rain

Acid rain

Slightly acid rain

Areas which could have problems in the future

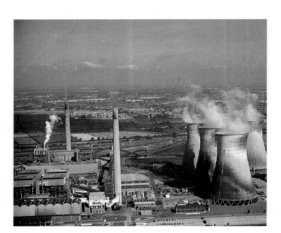

▲ **Coal-fired power station** in the English Midlands. Steam rises from the cooling towers (right), but the smoke from the chimneys (left) causes most of the air pollution. The big coal "stockpile" can be seen beyond the cooling towers. We can't see the air pollution – but it's there, and some of it is carried by the wind to other European countries. The UK emits more sulfur into the atmosphere than any other country in Europe.

▶ **Air pollution in Africa.** This copper works at Rokana in Zambia causes lots of air pollution. Molten slag is being tipped from a railroad truck, so there is damage to the land as well as the air.

POLLUTION ISN'T NEW!
People who lived near smoky chimneys during the Industrial Revolution breathed in polluted air every day. As recently as 1951 nearly 3,000 people died from a killer "smog" in London.

WHAT IS THE OZONE HOLE?
The "ozone hole" high above Antarctica is getting bigger. The "hole" lets more ultra-violet radiation reach the Earth – leading to more skin cancers in people, and slower growth in plants. The main cause seems to be chlorofluorocarbon gases ("CFCs"). That's why scientists want CFCs banned.

▶ **We are polluting** our rivers and seas – and there are new problems almost every month. Rivers bring more and more pollution to the coast – and currents move it to new areas of the oceans. Raw sewage is still pumped into the sea in many countries, some of which are the "advanced" nations. Some of the "solutions" cause more problems: the chemicals that are supposed to deal with oil pollution can sometimes cause even more damage to ocean waters, coastlines and fish than the oil itself does.

WATER POLLUTION

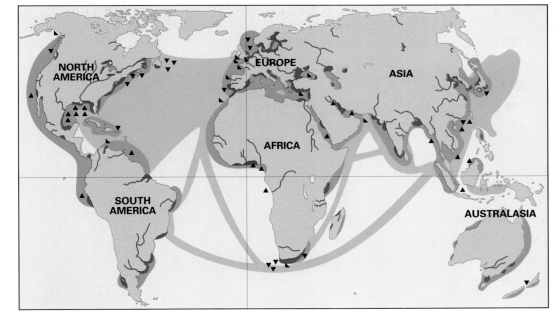

■	Badly polluted sea areas and lakes	◣	Big oil tanker spills
▨	Other polluted sea areas and lakes	▲	Big oil rig blowouts
▧	Oil pollution from ships	▽	Waste from towns and factories dumped at sea
		—	Badly polluted rivers

Are these pictures of the same river?
Yes, they are! It is the river Anker, in the English Midlands. The two photographs were taken quite close to each other.
◀ **Upstream** of a sewage outflow the water is clear, and the waterweeds grow well. This is how a river ought to be.
▶ **Downstream** of a sewage outflow there is foam from detergents, and lots of other pollution. And the river is smelly too! The cause is people – we seem to prefer cheaper bills to cleaner rivers.

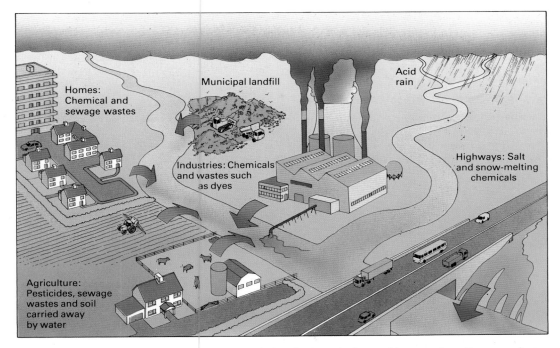

Most of the problems shown above COULD be dealt with. It would cost a lot of money, but it would be worth it in order to protect our rivers – and therefore our oceans.

◀ **The causes of river pollution**
The diagram shows that almost everything adds to river pollution.
• From homes, everything we put down the drain is only partly "cleaned" in a sewage works – and then goes to the river.
• Rainwater falling on garbage dumps may collect chemicals.
• On farmland, rainwater can pick up pesticides and chemical fertilizers.
• Poisons from factories go into the river (see photograph on page 66).
• Acid rain makes all the water that comes to the river more acid than it used to be.
• Even roads add to river pollution: the chemicals put on winter roads help the ice and snow to melt faster.

★ There's more about pollution on pages 21 (Greenhouse Effect), 26 (Scandinavia), 36 (Mediterranean), 38 (Eastern Europe), 48 (China), 49 (Japan) and 67 (USA).

Using up resources

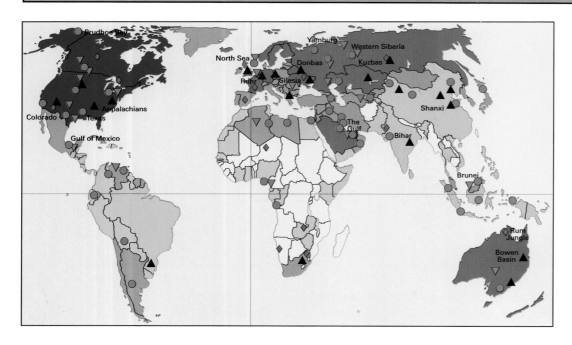

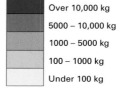

◀ *Who uses the energy?* This map shows the average amount of "energy" used per person per year by each country in the world. The darker the color on the map, the more energy is used per person. The people of the rich countries use most energy — and cause most pollution. The countries colored dark brown use over 100 times more energy per person than the pale yellow countries. All the energy used has been "converted" into kilograms (.45 lbs.) of coal.

Over 10,000 kg	**MAIN AREAS OF PRODUCTION**
5000 – 10,000 kg	● Oil
1000 – 5000 kg	▽ Natural gas
100 – 1000 kg	▲ Coal
Under 100 kg	◆ Uranium *(the fuel used for nuclear power)*

Energy is the source of power for heat, for transport and above all for industry. Most energy used by us is "non-renewable": coal, oil and natural gas. These are "fossil fuels" made long ago — and they cannot last for ever or be renewed. Also, they cause many of the world's pollution problems — see pages 16–17 and 20–21.

The more energy we save, the less pollution we cause. The darker colors on the map show what are called the "developed" countries — but some people say that they use up too much energy producing things that are not really needed. And in doing so they produce most of the world's "greenhouse gases."

▼ *The balance of world energy.* Each square on the "maps" below shows 1% (one-hundredth) of the world's energy. The map on the left shows a big Middle East, because it produces so much oil. But in the map on the right, the Middle East is quite small because it uses little energy. Compare Japan — tiny on the left map, and bigger than the whole of Africa on the right! Japan uses vast amounts of energy in its homes and factories, even though it is not in the "top ten" countries for energy used per person. North America uses over a quarter of all the energy used in the world — yet it has less than a tenth of the population. The USA uses more energy than any other nation.

▼ *A vegetable oil factory* in West Africa. But what type of energy is being used? You'll never guess! So the answer is somewhere on page 19....

PRODUCING WORLD ENERGY

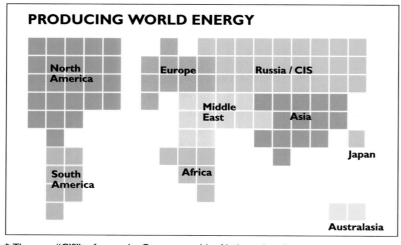

North America

Europe

Russia / CIS

Middle East

Asia

Japan

South America

Africa

Australasia

USING WORLD ENERGY

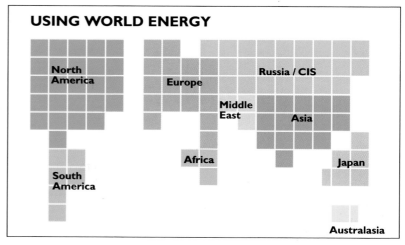

North America

Europe

Russia / CIS

Middle East

Asia

Africa

Japan

South America

Australasia

* The term "CIS" refers to the Commonwealth of Independent States, which was formed after the breakup of the USSR in 1991.

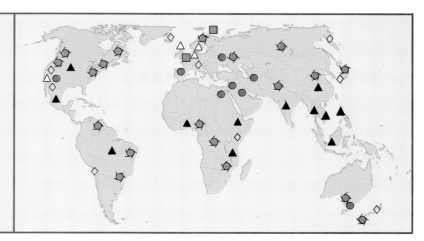

RENEWABLE ENERGY RESOURCES
(% of world total)

Hydroelectricity ⤸		Fuelwood ▲	
1. USA	14%	1. India	14%
2. Canada	12%	2. China	11%
3. Russia etc	11%	3. Indonesia	10%
4. Brazil	9%	4. Brazil	9%
5. China	6%	5. USA	7%

Other main renewable energy resources

Geothermal	◇	Wind	△
Tidal	◼	Solar	●

▲ **Renewable energy.** *The map shows six "renewable" types of energy, using the power of the sun, the tides and the wind, geothermal energy and firewood (see "biomass," below). The best-known type of renewable energy is hydroelectric power, using the power of falling water. "HEP" has many benefits, but dams and lakes still produce some problems.*

▲▶ **"Biomass"** *means anything that grows which can be used for energy, such as timber (above, in Ghana) or charcoal (right, for cooking in Zambia). Wood can be grown for fuel as a crop. But in places where collecting firewood is destroying bush or forests, there can be major problems. Other types of biomass are sugarcane waste changed into fuel for cars, as in Brazil. Or even peanut shells! (See opposite page, at a groundnut oil factory in The Gambia.)*

▲ **Wind power.** *This windpump in northern Kenya lifts water from below the ground for people, animals and crops. Wind power is free and does not pollute the air: it's a great source of energy. But it can't work everywhere, and is limited in power.*

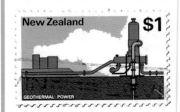

GEOTHERMAL ENERGY. The New Zealand stamp shows a pipe going down into the hot rocks below the surface. Another pipe leads to the power station (left). The photograph from the Kenyan rift valley shows that it's more complicated than that. This place is called "Hell's Gate." Geothermal power is a great source of renewable energy for countries where such heat is near the Earth's surface.

SOLAR POWER has long been used for making raisins (sun-dried grapes) and for getting salt (seawater evaporated by the sun). Now the sun's rays can be used to make electricity too.

* **MORE ABOUT ENERGY:** see pages 30, 33 & 55 (hydroelectric power), 90 (solar power), 30 (tidal power), 30 & 90 (wind power), 16 & 21 (coal-fired power stations), and 30 & 38 (nuclear power).

The Greenhouse Effect

The "Greenhouse Effect" is the name given to the theory that polluted air is causing the world to get warmer – "global warming." In a garden greenhouse, light energy from the sun comes in through the glass and is changed into heat energy. The glass traps most of the heat inside, so the greenhouse gets hotter and hotter.

In our "world greenhouse," similar factors are at work. The increase of air pollution seems to be making a denser layer of pollution in the atmosphere. Light from the sun still passes through and the light is still changed into heat. But more and more heat is trapped, so the world may be getting hotter.

▼ *This satellite image shows ten threats to our planet – all caused by air pollution. These dangers exist in many places, apart from the examples that are shown. It's a beautiful world, but...*

1. North Atlantic storms ... *could be more severe and there would be more hurricanes.*

2. North Sea coasts. *UK and the Netherlands could be at risk from rising sea levels.*

3. Slopes of the Alps. *Will there be enough snow for the skiers?*

4. Grainlands of Eastern Europe *could be threatened by drought.*

5. Nile Delta, Egypt. *Millions of people could be at risk from a rise in sea level.*

▼ **CARBON DIOXIDE**

(million tons per year)

Fuel burning

Deforestation

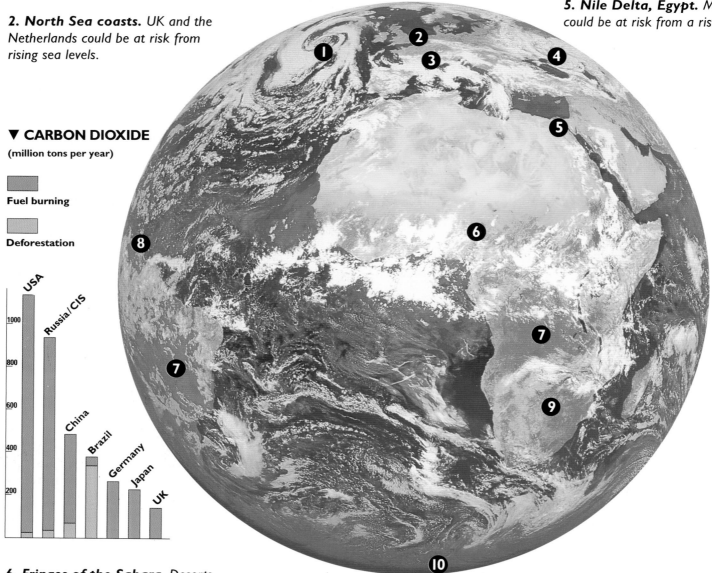

USA
Russia/CIS
1000
China
800
Brazil
Germany
600
Japan
400
UK
200

6. Fringes of the Sahara. *Deserts could spread even faster, and hundreds of thousands of people could die.*

7. Tropical rain forests. *Clearing the jungle is increasing the Greenhouse Effect.*

8. Coral islands of the Caribbean *could be destroyed by rising sea levels and fiercer hurricanes. Some small islands might vanish.*

9. Southern Africa. *The corn harvest could be threatened by drought.*

10. Antarctica. *Melting ice sheets would cause rising sea levels.*

THE GREENHOUSE EFFECT

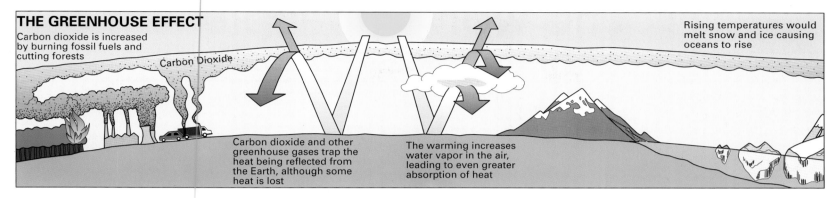

Carbon dioxide is increased by burning fossil fuels and cutting forests

Carbon Dioxide

Rising temperatures would melt snow and ice causing oceans to rise

Carbon dioxide and other greenhouse gases trap the heat being reflected from the Earth, although some heat is lost

The warming increases water vapor in the air, leading to even greater absorption of heat

▲ **How it works.** The main causes of the Greenhouse Effect are all linked with air pollution. When forests are cut down and destroyed (see page 74) more pollution stays in the air because fewer trees mean that less of the harmful carbon dioxide can be absorbed from the atmosphere.

▼ **Heating the greenhouse.** One of the main causes of the Greenhouse Effect is industrial pollution. This billowing smoke is from a coal-fired works. But many other types of factories add to air pollution.

▶ **Global "warning"!** The graph shows how serious the problem is. If air pollution continues to grow fast, scientists estimate that the world will get hotter and hotter (see the red line). The great need is to cut pollution, so that the change is not so fast (see the black line).

Cars and trucks are a major cause of air pollution. There are more of them every year. We all fall in love with toy cars before we understand the problems they cause — and adults STILL "worship" them! ▼

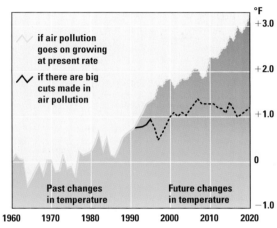

°F

if air pollution goes on growing at present rate

if there are big cuts made in air pollution

+3.0

+2.0

+1.0

0

−1.0

Past changes in temperature

Future changes in temperature

1960   1970   1980   1990   2000   2010   2020

◀ **Massive flooding** will result worldwide if a warmer Earth makes the ice sheets melt more quickly. This flood isn't too serious — but what will happen to the world's seaports?... to coastal cities?... and to hundreds of millions of people who live on the deltas of the great rivers? (See page 46.)

▶ **A warmer world** could be good news to some people. This vineyard in Norfolk, England, is only 13° away from the Arctic Circle: warmer summers would help the grapes a lot. But in many other places, farmland could be destroyed by drought.

The world's people

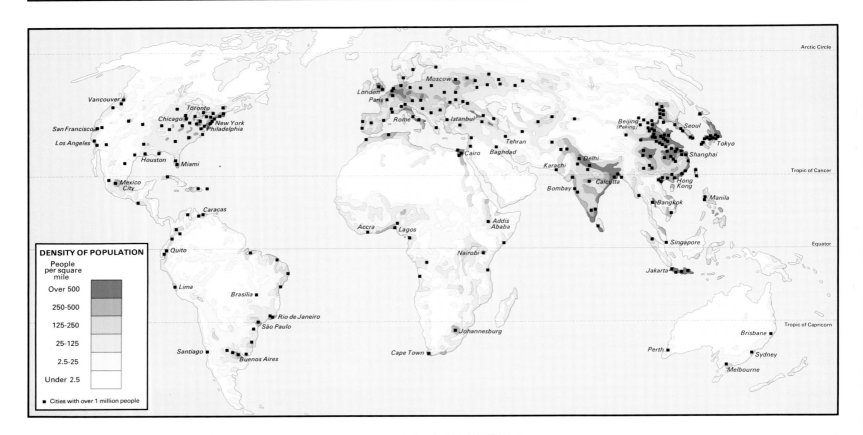

DENSITY OF POPULATION

People per square mile

	Over 500
	250-500
	125-250
	25-125
	2.5-25
	Under 2.5

■ Cities with over 1 million people

Most deserts on the map are almost empty of people (of course!) but many northern parts and forest areas also have few people. Perhaps the world is not as crowded as you thought. Population is a big problem for the environment, but is it the biggest? The people who use up most resources, and who create the most pollution, are from the rich countries, not the poor people. . . .

OF ALL THE WORLD'S PEOPLE...
- One in four lives in China.
- One in four lives in India, Russia or USA.
- One in four lives in the other 14 countries numbered on the "map" below.
- That's three-quarters of the world's people – in only 18 countries.
- The remaining quarter of the total is shared between 150 other countries.

NUMBERS OF CHILDREN
The Indian government has been encouraging parents to have only two children. In China, for years the government said "one child is enough."

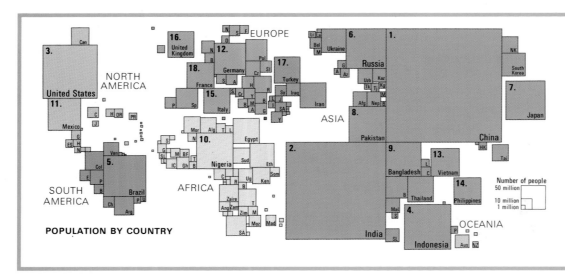

POPULATION BY COUNTRY

THIS SPECIAL "MAP" shows the size of the *population* of each country in the world. The bigger the square, the bigger the population. Huge countries with small populations, such as Australia and Canada, look smaller than small countries with big populations, such as Japan or Bangladesh. There are lots of surprises! Look how small the Middle East is, except for Turkey and Iran. Most African countries have small populations too, apart from Nigeria, Egypt and Ethiopia. The numbers on the "map" rank the "top 18" countries by the size of their population.

▲ **Singapore** is very crowded, with over 12,510 people per square mile. But the population is growing at a "safe" 1% a year.

▼ **Kenya** has only 126 people per square mile, but the population is growing very fast: over 3% a year. At this rate it will double in about 20 years. So how can there be enough jobs when these village children leave school?

DID YOU KNOW? The world's population is growing each year by more than the total present population of Britain. Yet some European countries, such as Denmark and Hungary, have "zero" growth of population.

▲ **A rider in Mongolia,** central Asia. Mongolia is the "emptiest" country in the world, with fewer than five people per square mile. Yet it is a neighbor of China, which has over a billion people.

▼ **The population graph** shows that the world's total number of people is approaching six billion. We reached:
1 billion in 1830.
2 billion in 1925 (after 95 years)
3 billion in 1960 (after another 35 years)
4 billion in 1975 (after only 15 years)
5 billion in 1988 (only 13 years) — and
8 billion is estimated for the year 2020.
The biggest overall growth is in Asia, but the fastest growth rates are in Africa, in poor countries least able to feed and clothe their people. While the population has doubled in 40 years, some of the Earth's rain forests have been halved and some animal species have been "decimated" — cut to only one-tenth or less of their numbers. There are signs that the growth in population will slow down some time in the next century — but will it be too late?

10,000 million people
9000
8000
7000
6000
5000
4000
3000
2000
1000

South Asia
East Asia
Australasia
Africa
South America
North America
USSR
CIS
Europe

Year
1750 1775 1800 1825 1850 1875 1900 1925 1950 1975 2000 2025 2050

Europe is the world's smallest continent. It is also the most crowded, so there are extra pressures on the environment and also many pollution problems. The political map shows how many countries there are – but they try to cooperate to solve problems. Pollution in the seas of Europe is a major concern: rivers carry contaminated water to the Baltic Sea in the north and to the Mediterranean Sea in the south... and both have only narrow exits.

► *The "natural vegetation"* map shows how varied the landscapes of Europe are. There is still forest, grassland and "scrub" (bushes), despite hundreds of millions of people.

Countries
Scale 1:35 000 000
0   200   400   600miles

▲ *Seals* near the Wadden Sea, off the Netherlands – part of the North Sea. Seals are good swimmers but they can only move slowly on land with their flippers. Sadly they are threatened by pollution and by a killer virus – another reason for reducing pollution. Governments have meetings about the North Sea, but it remains one of the world's most polluted waters.

PUZZLE STAMP FROM "HELVETIA." This slogan about the environment is in three languages:
- Which three languages?
- Can you understand the slogan?
- What country is Helvetia?
- What do the four pictures mean?
- Which is the "odd one out"? (Answers on page 96.)

LIFE AND DEATH IN THE FOREST
◄ **A tree dies,** and the fallen tree trunk becomes the home of fungi. But the seeds of other trees take root nearby and show their first leaves – **so the forest lives on.**

► **Native hardwoods,** such as these beech trees, are much less common in Europe than they used to be. Most of the hardwoods were felled long ago for building houses, horsecarts and ships. Now Europe imports millions of hardwood trunks from the tropics.

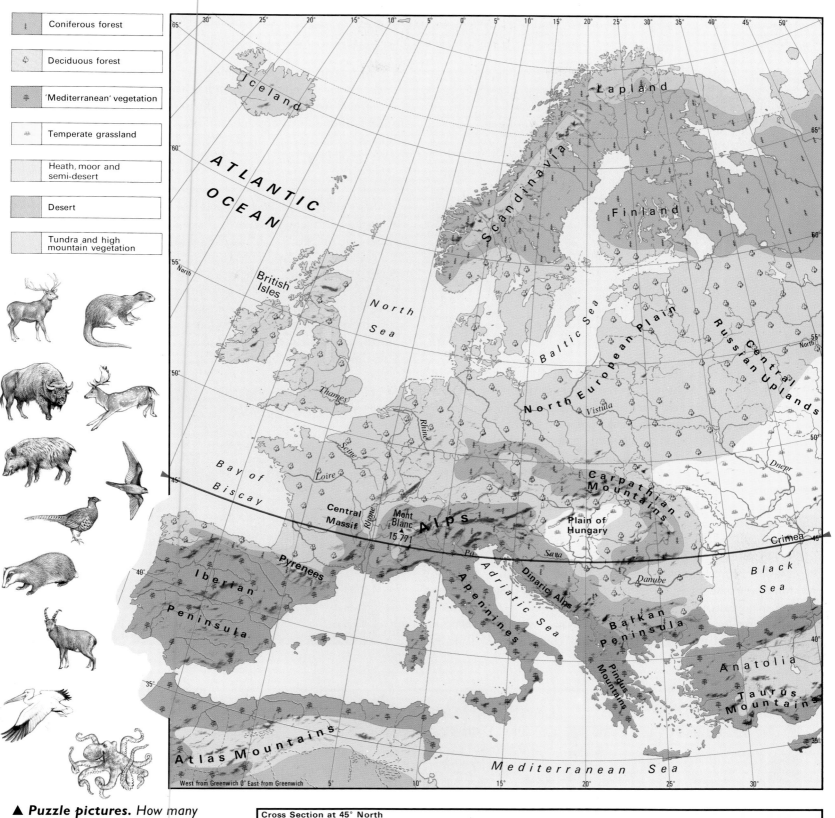

Legend:

- Coniferous forest
- Deciduous forest
- 'Mediterranean' vegetation
- Temperate grassland
- Heath, moor and semi-desert
- Desert
- Tundra and high mountain vegetation

Map labels:

ATLANTIC OCEAN

Iceland

Lapland

Scandinavia

Finland

British Isles

North Sea

Baltic Sea

North European Plain

Russian

Central Uplands

Thames

Vistula

Dnepr

Rhine

Seine

Loire

Bay of Biscay

Carpathian Mountains

Plain of Hungary

Central Massif

Rhone

Mont Blanc 15 771

ALPS

Po

Sava

Danube

Crimea

Pyrenees

Iberian Peninsula

Apennines

Adriatic Sea

Dinaric Alps

Balkan Peninsula

Black Sea

Pindus Mountains

Anatolia

Taurus Mountains

Atlas Mountains

Mediterranean Sea

West from Greenwich 0° East from Greenwich

▲ **Puzzle pictures.** *How many animals, birds and fish can you name?* (Answers on page 96.)

▶ **Cross section of Europe.** *The steepness has to be exaggerated, but the basic comparison is correct.*

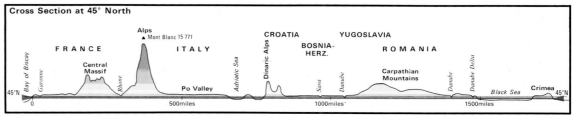

Cross Section at 45° North

FRANCE — Central Massif — Garonne — Rhone — Alps ▲ Mont Blanc 15 771 — ITALY — Po Valley — Adriatic Sea — Dinaric Alps — CROATIA — BOSNIA-HERZ. — YUGOSLAVIA — Sava — Danube — ROMANIA — Carpathian Mountains — Danube — Danube Delta — Black Sea — Crimea

Bay of Biscay

45°N   45°N

0   500miles   1000miles   1500miles

Scandinavia

◀ *A **reindeer** grazing in summer. The snow has melted, and reindeer enjoy eating the moss and lichens. But even in this remote part of northern Scandinavia the mosses have been polluted by fallout from the Chernobyl nuclear disaster (see page 38). Many other species of animal have adapted to survive in the harsh conditions, from wolves to lemmings.*

AN INTERNATIONAL PROBLEM . . .

Much of southern Scandinavia is covered by coniferous forests (see map on page 25). This is both a good wildlife habitat and a source of work for people: there are saw mills and woodpulp and paper factories. But acid rain is causing many of these trees to die. The Swedes say that coal-fired power stations in Britain are the main cause of the problem (see page 21). This is another example of pollution caused by one country harming another. The closeup picture shows that there is still some new growth on this spruce tree, but it is damaged and will probably die soon. Millions more will perish unless the air pollution is cut.

Scandinavia is the name for Norway, Sweden, Denmark, Iceland and Finland. Most people in these countries are quite rich. They use lots of oil for heating in the cold northern winters and plenty of gasoline for traveling. Even so, these countries are very keen on protecting the environment and stopping pollution – and the rest of the world can learn some lessons from Scandinavia. They have some advantages to start with: the mountains of Norway and Sweden are ideal for hydroelectric power, which does not pollute the air.

The Baltic Sea is shared by three Scandinavian countries and six other countries. (Can you name them? Answer on page 96.) All the nine countries pollute the sea. The Baltic has only narrow outlets to the North Sea, so pollution tends to stay inside it. The three Scandinavian Baltic countries are keen to cut pollution – but it is hard for them to persuade the other six countries to close down the factories that cause most of the problems.

Did you realize that the north of Norway, Sweden and Finland is further north than Iceland? Despite its "cold" name, Iceland is actually outside the Arctic Circle.

GLACIERS TODAY . . .

◀ **Stop! Danger!** Big blocks of ice may fall off the Nigard glacier in the mountains of Norway. The boy here *has* stopped; he helps you to see how big the glacier is.

▶ **In the past,** glaciers dug deep valleys in the hard rock and also made the fjords of the Norwegian coast. You can see the steep sides of the fjord. There is no road, but boats can travel safely on the deep sheltered water. This boat is going to Flam, on the Sogne Fjord.

. . . AND LONG AGO

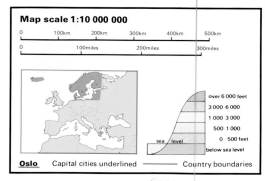

Map scale 1:10 000 000

over 6 000 feet
3 000-6 000
1 000-3 000
500-1 000
0-500 feet
sea level
below sea level

Oslo — Capital cities underlined —— Country boundaries

ÍSLAND

REYNIVIDUR SORBUS AUCUPARIA AR TRÉSINS 1980
ÍSLAND 120

ÍSLAND
6,50

TREELESS TUNDRA

It is too cold and windy for trees to grow in the tundra landscape of Iceland, and only 1% of the land can be farmed. But there are small bushes that have lovely flowers and berries in summer. (By the way: "Island" on the stamps is Icelandic for "Iceland," not for island!)

▲ *Strokkur geyser. Iceland is a volcanic island, and the word "geyser" is actually an Icelandic word. Cool water meets hot rock and the water boils and spurts out. Some are piped for hot water. Others are linked to geothermal energy projects (see page 19).*

FROZEN SEAS. The Gulf of Bothnia and the Gulf of Finland freeze over in winter. Yet the Atlantic coast of Norway stays free of ice all year round, even north of the Arctic Circle, because of the influence of the "Gulf Stream." This ocean current of warm water begins its journey thousands of miles away in the Caribbean.

THE "BALTIC REPUBLICS" of Estonia, Latvia and Lithuania were separate countries from 1918 to 1940, but for the next 50 years they were part of the USSR. Now they have become independent again – and they want to cut the pollution from the factories that the government of the Soviet Union built on their land.

British Isles

There's plenty of beautiful scenery in Great Britain – but much of it is being spoiled. Even the National Parks have development problems, such as bigger quarries and new roads. In some areas, too many walkers (people who are seeking to *enjoy* the countryside) are actually eroding the footpaths. But there are lots of organizations that are working to conserve the environment and the plants and animals that are at risk. And (at last!) the government has agreed to cut pollution from power stations.

▼ *The map* shows several big estuaries – such as the Severn, Mersey and Humber. If one was "dammed," there would be:
● "Clean and green" tidal electricity (as in France – see page 30).
● A new road route.
● A safer area for water sports.
But estuaries are valuable for wildlife – the mud is specially important for wading birds and the salt marshes are valued by migrant birds. Most conservationists are against damming estuaries.

IRELAND deserves its title "the Emerald Isle": it is probably the greenest part of Europe. It has fewer environmental problems than Britain. There are fewer coal mines, factories and power stations – though the peat bogs (a fossil fuel) are disappearing fast. The two parts of Ireland – Ulster and the Republic – agree on the need to conserve the Irish environment.

▲ *A wild fox* ... in town at night! Some foxes have discovered that towns and suburbs can be good places to live. There's plenty of food and it can be less dangerous than guns and poisons on farms.

A FISHY TALE ...
The salmon on this 10p Irish coin suggests that there are still fine fish in the rivers and seas of Ireland.

Map scale   1:6 000 000

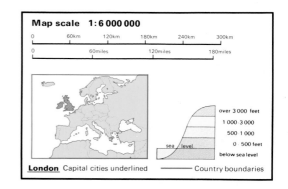

London Capital cities underlined   ——— Country boundaries

over 3 000 feet
1 000 – 3 000
500 – 1 000
0 – 500 feet
below sea level
sea level

WETLANDS FROM THE AIR

★ *More wetlands on pages 31 and 69* ★

◄ **It's not natural!** Some 800 years ago, people dug peat to burn on household fires. When flooded, they became the "Norfolk Broads," now home to many rare species of plants and insects. However, there are many man-made threats to the lakes, with nitrates from farms going into the water and tourist boats destroying riverbanks.

► **A salt marsh** beside the North Sea. The plants have adapted to survive in and out of water. So it's a special habitat – threatened by industry or by damming estuaries.

▲ *A beautiful coastline? Look again! There's lots of beautiful unspoilt countryside nearby – but waste from this Scottish coal mine near Edinburgh has been dumped on the coast. Even the seawater has changed color to a pale grayish blue from the chemical pollution being put into it.*

ANIMALS AT RISK

These conservation stamps show various endangered species and their threatened habitats in Britain.

The barn owl is threatened ▲ partly because old barns, its favorite habitat, are being pulled down.

▲ **The pine marten** (in an oak tree!) and **the wild cat** are rare sights in the Scottish Highlands. ►

◄ **The natterjack toad** lives mainly in sand dunes – a fragile coastal habitat that tourists and visitors can easily damage.

◄ *Development or devastation? A limestone quarry near Buxton, in the Derbyshire Pennines. Limestone is needed for steelworks and for cement. But this quarry is next to the beautiful Peak District National Park in the background: does it spoil the landscape too much? You can see how the planners made the quarry owner "hide" the works deep inside the quarry. Yet to work properly the quarry has to get bigger or close down. This is an example of a very common problem with the environment: how do we protect the countryside while still providing industry with the "raw materials" it requires from the Earth?*

France and Benelux

▲ **Old "windmills"** have been preserved in the Netherlands and tourists love to see them. Many were "windpumps" — they used natural power to raise water from the marshes up into the rivers. Most people thought wind power had no future. . . .

▲ **New "windmills"** are being built in many places in the Benelux countries — not to mill grain or pump water, but to generate "clean and green" electricity. These aerogenerators are beside a canal near Den Helder, in the Netherlands.

This page looks at different types of power being used in France and the Benelux countries. Much coal and oil is being used as well, of course. And in the Alps and Pyrenees, hydroelectric power makes good sense: page 33 shows a dam for "HEP."

All forms of power cause some problems to the environment. A successful protest by conservationists stopped a new dam for hydroelectric power being built in the upper Loire valley. Even though this would be "clean" power, they felt that flooding the valley would destroy valuable habitats of plants and wildlife, as well as good farmland and beautiful scenery. Perhaps there needs to be more emphasis on *saving* energy rather than producing more power?

▲ **Tidal power in France.** ▶
The river Rance estuary has been dammed, and the falling water is used for "clean" electricity. The water level is higher on the left of the barrage (above) at high tide, and higher on the right at low tide. But tidal power can cause problems for wildlife.

◀ **A nuclear power station** on the river Loire, with steam billowing out of cooling towers. France has built many nuclear plants, and over half its electricity now comes from nuclear sources. The country has very little oil, so it seemed a good decision because it saved buying foreign fuel. But more and more people are now worried about the safety of such stations after the Chernobyl disaster of 1986 (see page 38).

2.5 MILLION ACRES PLANTED

... with about a hundred million trees! It sounds good news, but it may not be such good news after all. The stamp shows a big bulldozer removing all the plants that were growing. Most of the new trees are conifers, planted close, and this is not as suitable for most wildlife as the broadleafed forest.

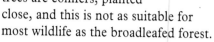

▼ **Storks nesting** on a rooftop in Alsace in eastern France. You can see three baby chicks in their nest. These big migrant birds can nest safely because everyone in the village has agreed not to disturb them!

▼ **France has wetlands too!**
The postage stamp of the area called "La Brenne" (square D4) shows a shallow lake with reeds and broadleafed forest – an important area for wildlife. This has now been set aside from development as a conservation area. France also has coastal wetlands like Les Landes (C5) and the Camargue (F6).

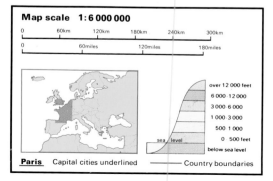
Map scale 1:6 000 000

0 60km 120km 180km 240km 300km
0 60miles 120miles 180miles

over 12 000 feet
6 000·12 000
3 000·6 000
1 000·3 000
500·1 000
0·500 feet
sea level
below sea level

Paris Capital cities underlined —— Country boundaries

FRENCH COINS. The 2-franc coin shows olives from the south of France, and oak leaves with acorns from the north. **Sowing seed by hand** (right) is called "broadcasting," but today most French farmers use expensive machinery.

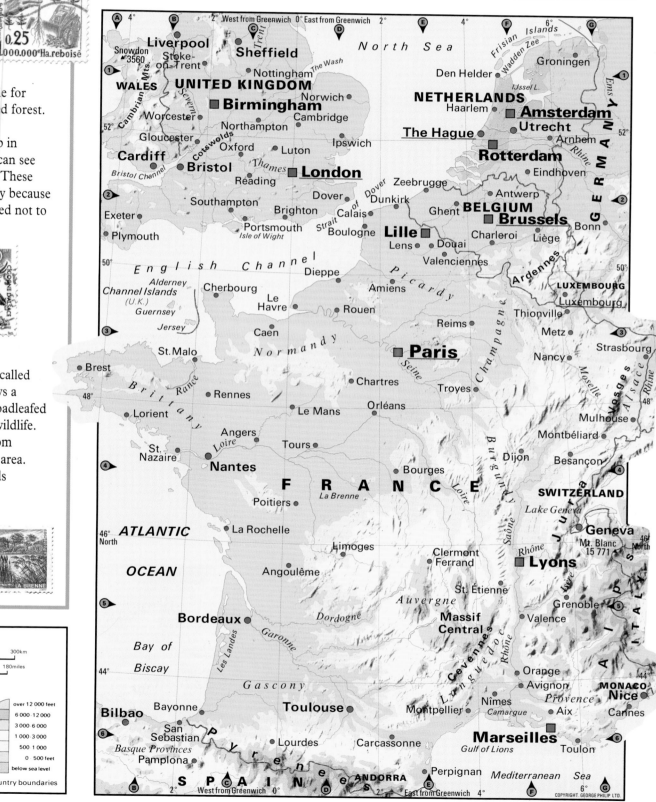

Germany and the Alps

Germany stretches from the Alps in the south, to the North Sea and the Baltic Sea in the north. There is a lot of beautiful unspoilt countryside: the picture below shows peaceful farmland as well as the Rhine Gorge. But there is also a lot of pollution. Some of the pollution in western Germany has been dealt with: coal mines have closed, and waste tips have been landscaped into parks and even ski slopes, but the rivers still carry too much harmful material. German cars now have strict pollution controls – but the big powerful engines of Mercedes, BMW and Audi cars still use a great deal of petrol.

In the eastern parts of Germany, industrial pollution is much worse (see bottom picture). Factories are being cleaned up or closed down, but the damage to the environment will last for many years to come. Some of Germany's rivers carry pollution that comes from other countries "upstream," so agreements are very important.

Map scale 1:6 000 000

| 0 | 60km | 120km | 180km |

| 0 | 60miles | 120miles |

over 6 000 feet
3 000 · 6 000
1 000 · 3 000
500 · 1 000
0   500 feet
below sea level

—— Country boundaries
Berlin Capital cities underlined

SCHÜTZT
DIE
NATUR!

. . . but what does the slogan mean?
(Answer on page 96.)

DEUTSCHE BUNDESPOST

IO

SCHÜTZT DIE NATUR

▲ **The Rhine Gorge** and Katz Castle, in western Germany. Forests cling to the steep valley sides. The Rhine carries more shipping than any other river in the world. It also carries all kinds of pollution downstream to the Netherlands and into the North Sea.

◄ **Bitterfeld** in eastern Germany – one of the most polluted towns in Europe. Two cyclists are passing a big smelly factory. A huge "clean up" program started after the two Germanies (East and West) united in 1990, following 45 years as separate countries with very different governments.

◄ GOOD NEWS in . . . . THE ALPS . . . . and BAD NEWS ▼

The pictures here sum up the joy and the sorrow of the Alps. It is a fragile environment: perhaps the steep slopes need a big label saying "HANDLE WITH CARE"?

The Alps are fold mountains shaped by the force of ice (glaciation) – and if people interfere too much there can be unexpected results (see picture below right).

◄ **The Alps** are the world's biggest winter sports area. These skiers have come by electric train to the ski slopes in the Berner Alps, Switzerland. The snow is smooth, the weather is good – it's perfect for a holiday. But. . .

► **Look at the devastation** when the snow disappears in summer. This digger has been making a new ski run in the French Alps. All the special alpine plants have been dug away.

◄ **Wild flowers** of every color decorate an alpine meadow. That's what the Alps should look like – but meadows like this are sadly being lost by thoughtless development.

► **Big new roads** were built to "Les Arcs" – a new ski village high in the French Alps. This upset nature's balance, and part of the mountainside slipped away. The new concrete walls are ugly and may not last long.

▲ *A hydroelectric dam for Tignes, in the French Alps. The Alps are ideal for "HEP": there is plenty of water from melting snow; steep valleys give a big drop of water; and there is strong rock to "tie" the dam to the valley sides. This electricity uses no fossil fuels, so there is no pollution. But it's not all good news – rare alpine plants and their habitats may be lost under the water of the new lake.*

▼ *The Alps are shared by several countries: Switzerland and Austria are small countries with a big area of the Alps. France and Italy are big countries with a small area of the Alps. Germany and Slovenia also have part of the Alps.*

And don't forget Liechtenstein – it's the only country that is 100% alpine. The Alps separate Italy from Germany – so there is a lot of freight that needs to cross the mountain frontiers. Switzerland and Austria want it to go by rail, not road.

Map scale 1:6 000 000

Western Mediterranean

PARCHI NAZIONALI is Italian for "National Parks." In the Abruzzo National Park, a few wild brown bears can still be found. They are less well known than American bears, because they are so rare. Once they were common – but people have killed bears for hundreds of years and now there are only six isolated groups left, in remote areas of Europe such as the Alps and the Pyrenees.

Italians still kill birds, however: every year many thousands of birds migrating across the Mediterranean Sea from Africa to Europe and back are shot by people with guns for "sport" – how cruel!

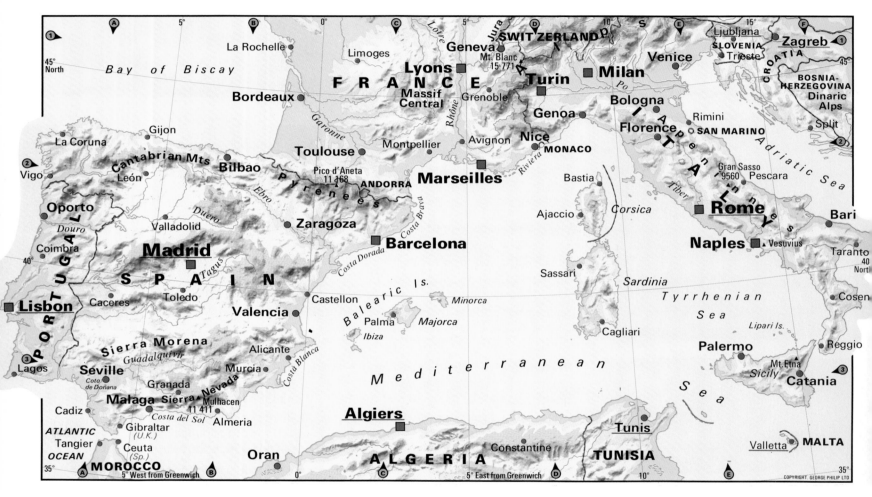

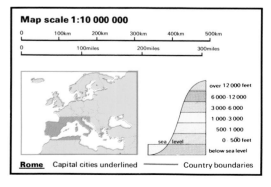

Map scale 1:10 000 000

0 100km 200km 300km 400km 500km

0 100miles 200miles 300miles

over 12 000 feet
6 000-12 000
3 000-6 000
1 000-3 000
500-1 000
0-500 feet
sea level
below sea level

Rome Capital cities underlined —— Country boundaries

LIFT UP THE OPPOSITE PAGE, AND YOU'LL SEE THE REST OF THE MEDITERRANEAN...

Every year millions of people visit the Mediterranean for a holiday. Most of them do not realize that the beautiful Mediterranean Sea is also a very polluted sea. Some pollution comes direct from coastal towns and factories. Lots more comes into the sea from big rivers like the Ebro (Spain), the Rhône (France) and the Po (Italy). Oil from ships is another major problem. But the good news is that the countries have now signed a convention against pollution of the water – and the situation should improve.

THE MEDITERRANEAN IS...

1 sea shared by:
2 island countries (Malta and Cyprus)
3 continents (Europe, Asia and Africa)
4 mainland Asian countries
5 African countries, and
6 mainland European countries.
That makes 17 countries – no wonder pollution is a problem.
Can you name them? Look at pages 34 and 37. (Answers on page 96.)

TOURISM: A blessing or a curse?

Tourism does not always ruin the landscape. In this new "tourist town" in Majorca, the high-rise hotels have been kept to a small area. In the foreground the olive groves and grass (for sheep) have not been damaged. Parts of the coastline have been protected here. Tall hotels take up much less space than lots of villas – though some people feel that they completely spoil certain parts of the coastline. And what happens if the tourists don't come to visit any more? Spain has more visitors per year than its own population, and only the USA earns more from tourism.

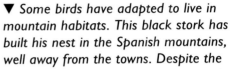

WETLANDS. . .

◄ **These little egrets** live near the sea in a wetland area: the Coto de Doñana in Spain. Wetlands in southern Europe are at risk for several reasons. Some people want to drain wetlands to build tourist hotels and villas. Others want to use these flat areas to grow irrigated crops. The pumping of water from underground, for tourists, changes some wetlands into dry areas. The best hope is to create nature reserves.

. . . and DRY LANDS

► **Goats** get hungry and thirsty in the long hot summers. Olives are a tasty meal – so it's worth them standing on their hind legs to get some juicy ones. But the farmer will not be pleased. . . .

◄ **The bark** has been taken from these trees in Portugal – but this isn't vandalism! The "cork oak" grows a tough bark, which is harvested to make corks for wine bottles. The bark protects trees from the hot, dry Mediterranean summers – but most cork oak trees survive this unusual "harvest." The cork oak is an "evergreen" tree, like many other trees in this part of the world.

▼ *Some birds have adapted to live in mountain habitats. This black stork has built his nest in the Spanish mountains, well away from the towns. Despite the tourist boom, huge areas of Spain remain unspoilt, away from the crowded coasts.*

CIGÜEÑA NEGRA · CICONIA NIGRA
ESPAÑA

WHERE EUROPE. . .

Try matching the satellite picture to the map. *Spain* is at the top (north); *Africa* is at the bottom (south); the *Atlantic Ocean* is on the left (west); the *Mediterranean Sea* is on the right (east). Five million years ago, "the Med" was dry – until the world's biggest waterfall from the Atlantic flooded it. There's still a strong current from the Atlantic in summer because so much Mediterranean water is evaporated.

. . .MEETS AFRICA

This photograph was taken by an astronaut in a spacecraft. This is a very important crossing point into Europe for migrating birds – as well as for people. Birds prefer to cross land, because they like to use pockets of warm rising air, called "thermals" – just as gliders do. Then the birds can glide for long distances, until they meet another "thermal." It's a lot less tiring than flying!

The Eastern Mediterranean has beautiful coastlines, beautiful mountains, beautiful cities – and horrible pollution in the air above cities, and in the seawater by the beaches. Yet it is still an area of the world that most people want to visit, because of the wonderful climate, the scenery and the historic places. So these two pages have both good news and bad news on them.

The Mediterranean is a busy sea. There are oil tankers from Libya, cargo ships from the Suez Canal, tourists from Greece and fishing boats from many countries.

◄ Turtles and tourists. *This loggerhead turtle will come onto the beach at Zakynthos (Zante), a Greek island, to lay eggs at night, and bury them in the sand. But tourists are there as well. When the eggs hatch, the baby turtles should run to the sea. But lights confuse them, and many run toward the lights and die before they reach the safety of the water. Turkey has now provided sanctuaries for the turtles.*

Did you know? "Mediterranean" means "Middle (medi) of the Land (terra)." It WAS the center of the world to Romans, who named it over 2,000 years ago.

◄ Limestone being made. *At the Krka falls in Croatia, the river deposits travertine – a freshwater limestone, something like the deposits you find in a pot. The water travels through limestone caves; then the lime is redeposited and makes these layers of rock. Lime-loving plants thrive in this lush wet area.*

▼ Limestone being destroyed. *The Parthenon in Athens, the capital of Greece, is one of many famous buildings ruined by acid rain from factories and by chemicals put into the air by cars and trucks. Today, scaffolding hides much of the Parthenon. This superb building has stood for over 2,400 years, but it is now threatened by the waste products of the modern world – despite the blue "picture postcard" sky.*

VENICE IN DANGER! They have canals instead of roads in Venice! The picture shows the Grand Canal, and houses where the door opens onto water (take care when you go out to take the dog for a walk!). Venice now faces many problems: the land is sinking very slowly, and high tides are more common, perhaps because of the Greenhouse Effect; so floods are now more likely; acid rain and pollution are ruining the stone of the famous buildings. A vast international project is trying to save the city, but the signs are not hopeful. Venice was once an important city, and it's now a very popular destination for tourists. Gondolas (see picture below) are still very popular – and they cause NO pollution and NO damage.

MALTA is an island country in the central Mediterranean (so it's on the map on page 34 as well as opposite). It is crowded compared to most European countries – yet even here there is countryside not yet overtaken by tourists. Malta is one of the main routes for birds migrating from Africa to Europe and back. The dove on this independence stamp is a symbol of freedom for everyone.

▼ **The map below** shows parts of three continents: Europe, Asia and Africa – there are parts of Libya and Egypt to the south. This is the only place in the world where three continents come close together. The area shown on the map uses ten different languages and five different alphabets – Roman, Cyrillic (Russian, Bulgarian), Greek, Hebrew and Arabic. So it's quite difficult for people to discuss environmental problems, and even harder to solve them.

MONK SEALS are becoming rarer in the Mediterranean each year, and there are now fewer than 1,000 left in the world. Fishermen fought them away from their areas, and tourists took over the beaches where they once lived. The great need now is for conservation areas to be set up – and the rules to be obeyed by all.

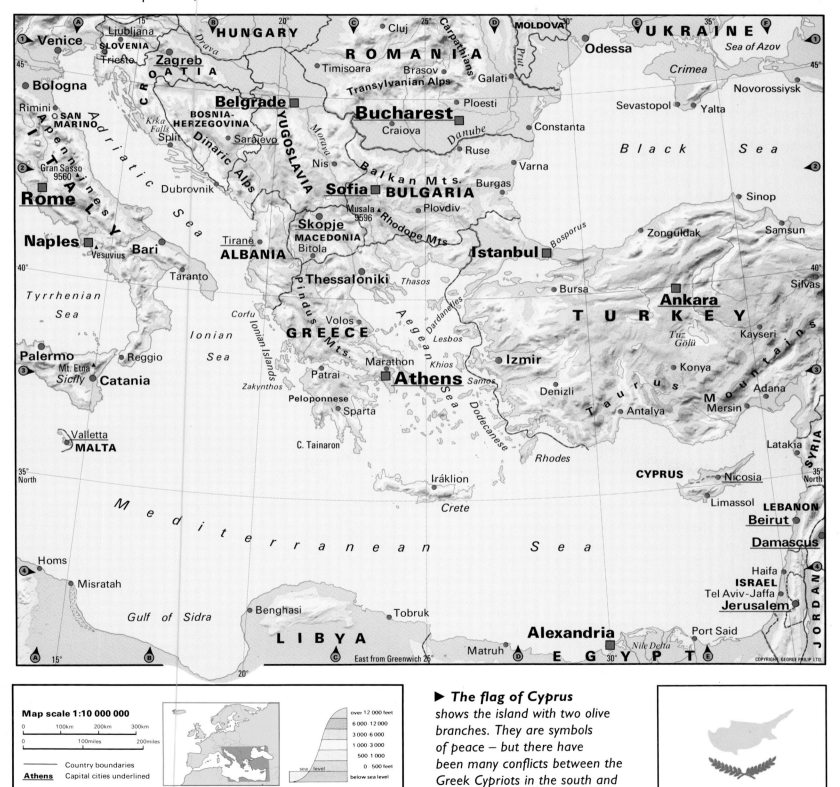

Map scale 1:10 000 000

| 0 | 100km | 200km | 300km |

| 0 | 100miles | | 200miles |

Country boundaries
Athens Capital cities underlined

over 12 000 feet
6 000–12 000
3 000–6 000
1 000–3 000
500–1 000
0–500 feet
sea level
below sea level

▶ **The flag of Cyprus** shows the island with two olive branches. They are symbols of peace – but there have been many conflicts between the Greek Cypriots in the south and the Turkish Cypriots in the north.

Eastern Europe

▶ *A rare photograph* taken after the world's worst nuclear accident at Chernobyl in April 1986. You can see the central building has collapsed – but you can't see the poisonous dust that covered a huge area around it. The dreadful effects of the explosion will be felt for years to come.

▼ *The Carpathian Mountains* in Romania are peaceful and very beautiful. This monastery has been in a quiet valley for hundreds of years. Crops and grass grow in the valley, and coniferous trees cover the hills. This area is typical of many of the hills and mountains of Eastern Europe. Yet in the industrial parts of Romania there is very bad pollution on a big scale.

▶ *The radioactive "fallout"* from Chernobyl spread far and wide – even to the Atlantic coast of Ireland in the west. This disaster has cost thousands of millions of roubles – and ruined the health of many people and animals. It has made several countries rethink their nuclear power program. After all, if this could happen in peacetime, much bigger disasters might happen if there were riots or wars. . . .

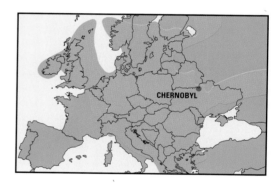

POLLUTION AND FARMLAND, side by side. This chemical factory at Plock, Poland, sends out poisonous fumes from its chimneys. Traditional farming methods are used beside the factory – but the poisons will enter the soil, and affect the crops. There is now a lot of concern about pollution from factories in Eastern Europe – pollution that has been belching out unchecked for many years. Some of the worst ones are closing down, but the unemployment that can result brings another set of problems. The governments and peoples of these countries have difficult decisions to make.

◀ **Amazing but true!** Poland was so proud of its smoky steelworks at Nowa Hute – in the country's industrial heartland near Krakow – that they even issued a postage stamp about it!

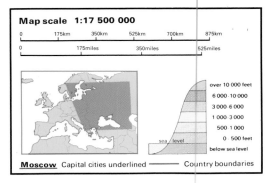

Map scale 1:17 500 000

0	175km	350km	525km	700km	875km
0	175miles	350miles		525miles	

over 10 000 feet
6 000 - 10 000
3 000 - 6 000
1 000 - 3 000
500 - 1 000
0 - 500 feet
sea level
below sea level

Moscow Capital cities underlined ——— Country boundaries

The map shows that most of Eastern Europe is lowland, but the Czech Republic, Slovak Republic and Romania are mainly mountainous. However, the highest point in Europe is in Russia: Mt. Elbrus in the Caucasus Mountains (18,481 feet) is much higher than Mont Blanc in the Alps (15,771 feet). Poland's rivers flow to the Baltic Sea, but the rivers of Hungary and Romania flow to the Black Sea.

ALPINE FLOWERS grow in the high mountains of the Tatransky Narodny Park (Tatra National Park), near the Polish border in the Slovak Republic. This one is called an edelweiss.

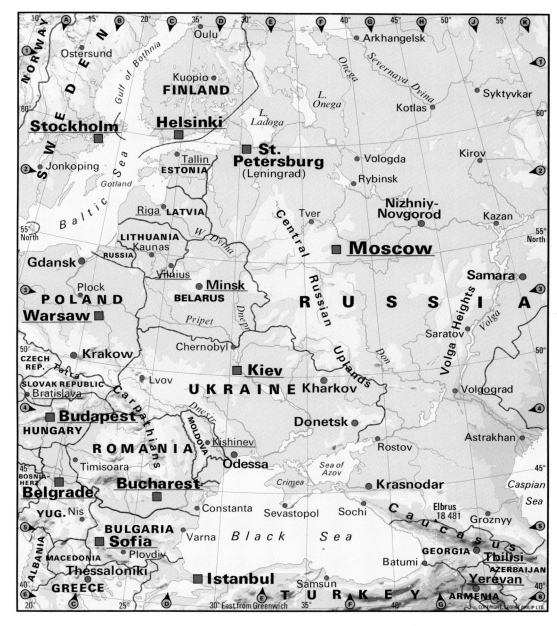

ZOOS: For or against?

These stamps from Poland show some of the wild animals and their babies in Warsaw Zoo: elephants, seals, polar bears and wild horses. Most capital cities in Europe have a big zoo, often one that was first opened many years ago. Children can see *real* wild animals: they are much more exciting than books or videos. And scientists can study the animals and sometimes help to preserve an endangered species. Some animals have to be kept in special conditions.

BUT it is very expensive to run a zoo. And is it unkind to keep wild animals in cages? Wildlife and safari parks let the animals roam far more. Winter in northern Europe is very cold – so is it unfair to keep elephants indoors, when the animals want to live in the conditions of their own hot countries? What do *you* think?

You can find pictures of each of these four animals in this atlas. In which countries are they seen? (Answers on page 96.)

ASIA

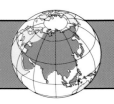

Asia is by far the largest continent in the world. It is the most varied continent too. It has nearly every kind of environment, from very hot areas to places with bitterly cold winters; from very dry places to some of the wettest places on Earth; and from the highest to the lowest places in the world (right). It also has the most crowded and the "emptiest" countries (see page 23).

The ten pages that follow explain some of the contrasts in Asia. The "political" map below shows that Russia, China and India are by far the biggest countries – but there are also lots of small nations, especially in Southwest Asia (the Middle East). Asia has over half the total world population – yet the map on page 22 shows that many parts have a low density of population.

▲ **HIGH. . .** This photograph of the Himalayas was taken by an astronaut in the *Columbia* spacecraft.
Can you spot:
- Snow-covered mountain ranges?
- Deep valleys between the ranges?
- Lowlands of the Indus plains?

The Himalayas are one of the world's greatest "wilderness" areas, and its melting snow keeps rivers flowing.

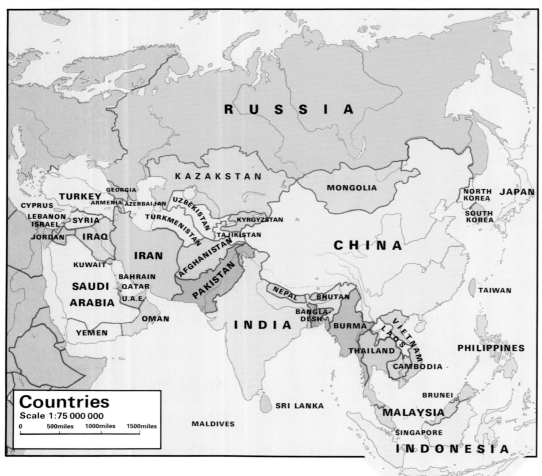

Countries
Scale 1:75 000 000
0   500miles   1000miles   1500miles

▼ **. . . AND LOW.** The lowest land in the world is on the shore of the Dead Sea, in the Middle East. The River Jordan flows into the Dead Sea but the hot sun evaporates water quickly – leaving thick salty water that even non-swimmers can easily float in.

CAN YOU NAME the other continents on the map above:
- To the west? (upper left)
- To the southwest? (lower left)

What continent would you meet if you:
- Went southeast of the map?
- Went beyond the top of the map?
- Went beyond the bottom of the map?

The small "globe" at the top of the page will help you. (Answers on page 96.)

JOURNEYS ACROSS ASIA

Imagine traveling east across Asia at 60° North – you would travel through 4,000 miles of forest, with some farmland. You would be in Russia, all the way from the Urals to the Pacific Ocean.

A journey at 30° North would be much more difficult (see the cross section). From the Arabian Desert, across the plateau of Iran, through barren mountains to the Indus valley; then over the Himalayas to reach the high plateau of Tibet; finally, down the Yangtze river valley to the ocean.

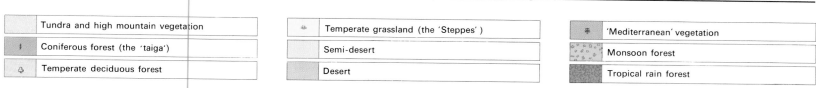

Tundra and high mountain vegetation	Temperate grassland (the 'Steppes')	'Mediterranean' vegetation
Coniferous forest (the 'taiga')	Semi-desert	Monsoon forest
Temperate deciduous forest	Desert	Tropical rain forest

ARCTIC OCEAN

Scandinavia

North European Plain

Ural Mountains

Ob

Yenisey

Siberia

Lena

Verkhoyansk Range

Kamchatka Peninsula

Mediterranean Sea

Black Sea

Caucasus
Mount Elbrus 18 481

Caspian Sea

Aral Sea

Lake Balkhash

Altay

Lake Baykal

Gobi Desert

Japan

Nile

Sinai

Syrian Desert

Plateau of Iran

Zagros Mountains

The Gulf

Pamir Mountains

Hindu Kush

Tien Shan

Kunlun Shan

Tibet

Huang He Hwang Ho

Chang Jiang Yangtze

East China Sea

PACIFIC OCEAN

Tropic of Cancer

Red Sea

Arabian Desert

Rub al Khali

Indus

Himalayas

Mount Everest 29 028

Thar Desert

Ganges

Brahmaputra

Mekong

China

Arabian Sea

Deccan

Bay of Bengal

South China Sea

Equator

INDIAN OCEAN

Malay Peninsula

Sumatra

Borneo

Indonesia

East from Greenwich

COPYRIGHT GEORGE PHILIP & SON LTD

Cross Section at 30° North

EGYPT | SAUDI ARABIA | IRAN | PAKISTAN | INDIA | CHINA

Himalayas
Brahmaputra
Tibetan Plateau
29 028 ▲ Mount Everest
Mekong
Chang Jiang (Yangtze)

Nile
Sinai
Nafud Desert
The Gulf
Plateau of Iran
Indus
Ganges
Chang Jiang (Yangtze)
East China Sea

30°N

1000miles | 2000miles | 3000miles | 4000miles | 5000miles

30°N

Giant Panda

RUSSIA AND NEIGHBORS

This area has every type of world environment, except tropical lands. It is such a huge country that the scale of this map has to be much smaller than for any other country (compare it with the map on page 39, which shows the western parts in more detail).

"Build more and more factories" was the main aim of the Communist government's five-year plans, but:

- Half the water sources are polluted.
- 100 towns have air pollution over ten times the accepted international limit.
- The Aral Sea, once the world's fourth biggest lake, is vanishing (see next page).
- Nuclear power was not safe (see page 38 for the Chernobyl disaster).
- The unique habitat of Lake Baykal, the world's deepest freshwater lake, is being damaged by chemical pollution.

But... the authorities are now trying to rescue the situation in many different ways.

▼ *The world's biggest forest is not the Amazon Forest. It is the "taiga," the coniferous forest of Russia. There are over 400,000 square miles of coniferous forest (far bigger than most large countries) and most of it has not been felled — yet. This summer view of a river on the Finland border would be snow-covered for months in winter.*

▲ **Bear facts:** the Latin name of the polar bear, which scientists use, is easier to read than the Russian name: *Thal* (Bear) *Arctos* (Arctic) *Maritimus* (Sea). It should really be called a "North Polar Bear" – they don't live in the Antarctic.

THE SIBERIAN TUNDRA

Siberia (below) has incredibly cold winters. In some places, the average January temperature is below −40° Fahrenheit. Yet these animals survive because the snow cover is thin and they can still find shrubs to eat below the snow. In summer, the tundra is marshy: the layer underneath the soil is still frozen so rainwater cannot soak in. It can be a colorful scene, in Scandinavia and North America as well as Siberia.

CITIES IN RUSSIA

There are bad pollution problems in several Russian towns and cities, like this factory in St. Petersburg (Leningrad). But it's not always as bad as it looks. It's a very cold winter day – so the steam and hot air make bigger "clouds" than they would on hot days.

The picture shows good news too: Russia has very good streetcars in many of its cities – cheap, frequent, quite fast, and safe. So there is much less pollution from cars and buses than in most Western European cities.

PICTURES THAT TELL A STORY
The Pamir Mountains (below) are much higher than the highest mountains in the Alps or the Rockies, or even the Andes – yet they are almost unknown to most people outside the area. From the snowy peaks on the border, at the western end of the "roof of the world," rivers flow all year. This is very useful, because these rivers flow northwest toward . . .

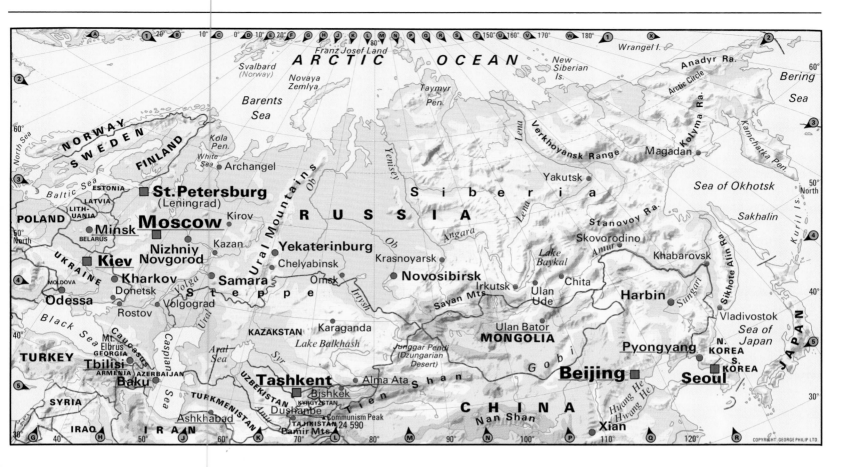

... the desert of central Asia. This desert (above) is as dry as the Sahara, so the Amu and Syr Rivers are vital. The cities get plenty of water, and huge irrigation schemes run by the government now allow semitropical crops such as cotton to be grown, because the "continental" type of summer here is really hot. It seemed an excellent project at the time, but everyone involved in the planning of the idea seemed to forget about one thing – the effect on ...

... the Aral Sea (below). The Amu and Syr rivers flow into the Aral Sea (map square J4) and they used to keep it full. But more and more water now flows into the irrigation channels, so less and less water reaches the Aral Sea, which has shrunk by a third. It's a huge disaster – and it's too late to rescue the fishing boats and the ships: they are stranded. Now the government is trying to increase the flow of the rivers again.

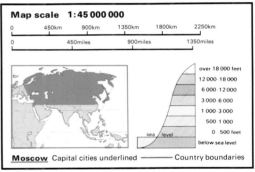

Map scale 1:45 000 000

| 0 | 450km | 900km | 1350km | 1800km | 2250km |

| 0 | 450miles | 900miles | 1350miles |

over 18 000 feet
12 000 - 18 000
6 000 - 12 000
3 000 - 6 000
1 000 - 3 000
500 - 1 000
0 - 500 feet
below sea level

Moscow Capital cities underlined ——— Country boundaries

SEABIRDS OF RUSSIA

Millions of seabirds live around Russia's 28,900-mile coastline. In summer, barnacle geese (left) breed on Novaya Zemlya (map square J1), and before winter comes they migrate to the salt marshes that border the North Sea. The Ross's gull (right) nests in swamps in Siberia.

Middle East

The Middle East is where three continents meet: Europe, Asia and Africa. So it is a very important area for people and also for plants and animals. This is where, long ago, people first learned to grow wheat and barley, and where cattle, sheep and goats became domesticated. Many wild animals that lived here in biblical times (such as lions and bears) were killed off many centuries ago. As the opposite page shows, the destruction still goes on.

▶ **The Arabian oryx** *looks at home here, among the desert shrubs of Oman. In fact, this was the home of the oryx before they were all shot by hunters. By 1972, every single oryx in Oman and Saudi Arabia had been killed.*

But this story has a happy ending: three oryx had been taken to Phoenix Zoo in Arizona. Zoo keepers cared for them well, and babies were born. In 1981, oryx were reintroduced into Oman and they are doing well. They are now a protected species, and hunting them is forbidden. Jordan and Saudi Arabia have also reintroduced this beautiful creature to the wild. The story of the oryx shows how cooperation between countries can save endangered species.

◀ **The artist** who painted Ramon Nature Reserve, in the Israeli desert, saw that the rock crystals reflected many different colors. The wide sandy "wadi" (dry valley) in the center contrasts with the distant mountains, which look blue and purple in the clear desert air.

▶ **The "Empty Quarter"** of Arabia is so empty that a large camel has been put on half the map on this stamp! Camels are still vital in the desert. Their broad feet cope well with soft sand, and the fat in their humps helps them to survive for long periods without water.

IT'S NOT ALL DESERT...

Lebanon is famous for its "cedars of Lebanon." These big, beautiful trees used to grow on the mountains, but very few are left now. The flag and the coins of Lebanon (below) show a cedar tree, with its big branches and broad trunk.

There are other non-desert areas. The world rainfall map on page 10 shows that much of Turkey has good rainfall. And the mountains of Yemen in the south of the area have enough rain for coffee to grow well there.

THE AMAZING DATE PALM

Most of the world's dates come from the Middle East: Iraq, Iran, Saudi Arabia, Yemen, Oman and the United Arab Emirates are all leading producers. The date palm (see pictures on pages 11 and 54) is specially adapted to the area's climate. All palms differ from other trees in that all the fronds grow from the top of the trunk. New fronds sprout from the top center. The trunk is made of the older palm fronds that died and broke off. So the tree trunk is fibrous and very different from the wood of other trees.

Date palms can provide shade for people and certain crops; the trunks are used for bridges over irrigation ditches and for houses; and the fronds give thatch and "straw" for the animals.

▼ **A market in Kayseri, Turkey.** There are lots of tomatoes and other fruit and vegetables for sale. In the background is a mosque, the place of worship for Muslims, and a mountain almost lost in the "heat haze."

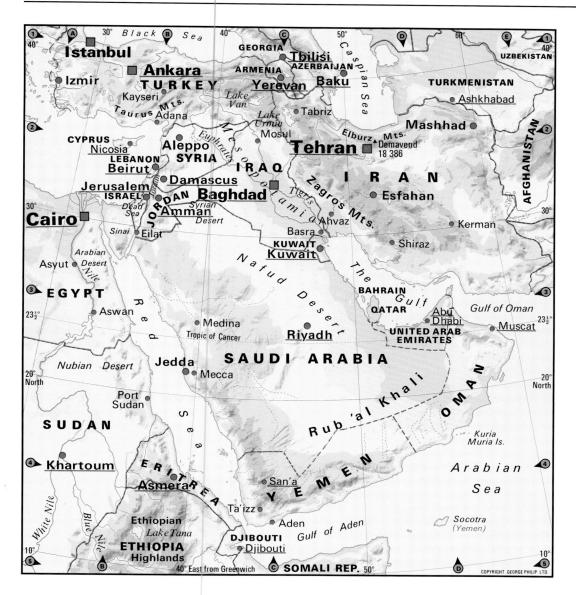

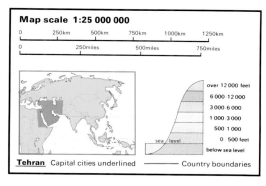

Map scale 1:25 000 000

| 0 | 250km | 500km | 750km | 1000km | 1250km |

| 0 | 250miles | 500miles | 750miles |

over 12 000 feet
6 000-12 000
3 000-6 000
1 000-3 000
500-1 000
sea level
0-500 feet
below sea level

Tehran Capital cities underlined — Country boundaries

▲ *The dugong or "sea cow."* One book calls the dugong "the sea's ugliest creature" – but some people think they are delightful! They feed on seaweed and sea grasses. Believe it or not, they are more closely related to elephants than to seals. In the Gulf, they were at risk from the terrible oil pollution caused during the Gulf War of 1991.

OIL: A blessing or a curse?

◀ **An oil rig in the desert.** Oil has made many countries in the Middle East rich. There are new roads and new irrigation projects to grow food, and many new schools and hospitals have also been built. But the oil has brought pollution to the air and to the seas. And some of the wealth has been used in bad ways – such as buying weapons for war.

▶ **An abandoned Iraqi tank** in Kuwait in 1991, in front of a burning oil well. Over 500 oil wells were set alight by the Iraqi forces, and thick black smoke covered hundreds of square miles for months. Oil spills in the Gulf threatened sea life and birds as well – both the residents and the migrants. Humans suffer too: the water supply of the Gulf states relies on desalinated seawater.

South Asia

India has more people than any other country, except for China: over 900 million people live there. Pakistan and Bangladesh are also in the "top ten" countries of the world for population, with over 100 million people each. So pressure on land is a real problem in many parts of South Asia.

But even here, some wildlife habitats are protected. There are still tigers and jungles, wetlands and unspoilt mountains, and even deserts as well. Look on the map for the tiny state of Bhutan high up in the Himalayas – it is probably the most unspoilt country in the world.

Today India has lots of modern industry. Sadly, such progress has brought new types of pollution. One night in 1984, poisonous gas leaked from the Union Carbide pesticides factory in Bhopal. Thousands of people died and tens of thousands of people were injured in the world's worst ever industrial accident.

It was a terrible example of the damage that pollution coming from lack of care can cause. And it brought to the attention of the world the way in which some of the companies based in the rich countries exploit the people of the poorer countries.

ENVIRONMENT: CAUSE AND EFFECT

The problem shown above is one of the main causes of the problem shown below right – even though the two photographs were taken hundreds of miles apart.

▲ *This hillside in Nepal has been terraced to try to prevent erosion. You can see large "steps" in the fields on the left. But, on the right, a big landslip has destroyed the land. Gullies will form – and the soil will be washed down by the rains into the rivers that flow into the Bay of Bengal.*

▶ *Bangladesh is a low-lying country at the delta of the Ganges and other rivers. It suffers from terrible floods. The rivers flood more often than before because there is*

more silt – caused by the erosion in the hilly areas shown above. There is also flooding caused by cyclones sweeping in from the sea. These storms seem to be getting worse, and more than 132,000 people died in one such storm in 1991.

THE MALDIVE ISLANDS are a group of low coral atolls in the Indian Ocean. The population of 220,000 is dependent mainly on fishing and tourism. But if the Greenhouse Effect does cause a rise in sea level, the whole country could vanish.

▲ **The tiger** nearly became extinct: the number in Asia dropped from 100,000 in 1939 to only 5,000 in 1970. But now they are protected from hunters. Some villagers near the tiger reserves get jobs and money to help with conservation work. So nowadays it is in everyone's interest to conserve the tiger and its habitat. The "core" (central) area of the tiger reserves is fully protected. Around each core there is a "buffer zone" where the villagers are allowed to collect firewood, wild fruit and bamboo for their homes. BUT poachers are still a threat to tigers.

WHY HUG . . . A TREE?
The "Chipko Movement" was formed by a group of women in Reni, northern India, who wanted to save their forest. So they hugged the trees when the lumberjack moved in, forming a human barrier. And it worked! They saved their trees, and people in other places followed their example.

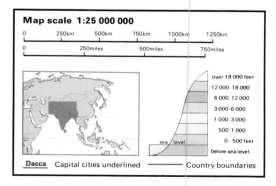

Map scale 1:25 000 000

| 0 | 250km | 500km | 750km | 1000km | 1250km |

| 0 | 250miles | 500miles | 750miles |

over 18 000 feet
12 000-18 000
6 000-12 000
3 000-6 000
1 000-3 000
500-1 000
0 - 500 feet
sea level
below sea level

Dacca Capital cities underlined ——— Country boundaries

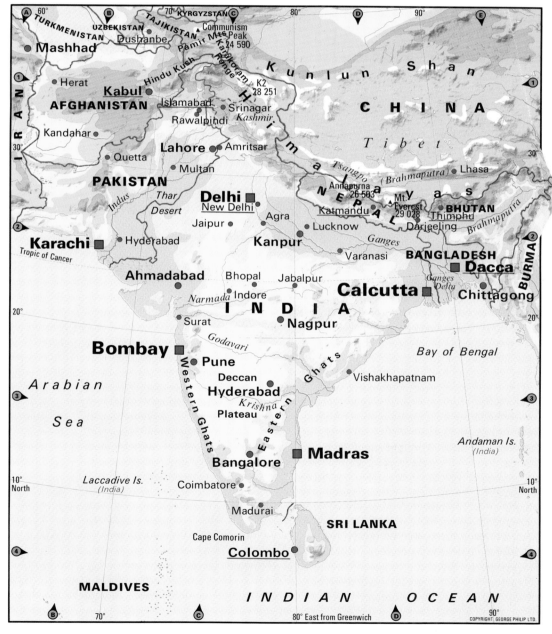

East Asia

◀ TWO ENDANGERED SPECIES ▶

◀ *Everyone loves pandas!* That's why WWF chose one for their logo. The remote mountains of southwest China are the home of the giant panda. Bamboo is a panda's favorite food. They can eat meat, too – but they are usually too slow to catch any! The panda is an endangered species partly because of the life cycle of the bamboo. This plant only comes into flower every 50 to 100 years, and then it dies: a whole area of bamboo can die at once. In the past, pandas could roam the mountains and valleys moving from one area of bamboo to another. Nowadays the few remaining pandas live in small areas of bamboo forest surrounded by farmland, so they find it hard to survive.

▶ *Mongolia* is home to the last wild horses in the world, Przewalski's Horse. They were once near extinction, but they have been successfully bred by zoos in Europe (see page 39). Now the United Nations and Mongolia have combined to reintroduce these horses to the Mongolian "steppes."

CHINESE PUZZLE

China is changing very fast, and each new development brings some benefit to the country and its people. But it usually brings problems too. Here are some of the main ones . . .

DEVELOPMENT	"FOR"	"AGAINST"
MORE coal mines	● Increased production ● Less need to import oil	■ More countryside destroyed ■ More carbon dioxide in the air
MORE factories	● Work for more people ● Better-paid jobs	■ More air pollution ■ More pollution of rivers
MORE fridges	● Food keeps better and longer ● Less food poisoning	■ More CFCs (see page 16) ■ More energy required
MORE tourists	● Foreign money comes in ● More jobs ● People understand China better	■ More traffic = more pollution ■ Development of unspoilt areas ■ More air-conditioning

▶ *Industry at Anshan, northeast China.* This steelworks uses lots of coal, and there are fewer controls over pollution than in most richer countries. China produces and uses huge amounts of coal, so this problem may get worse. But most Chinese people cause very little pollution: even today, most of them are farming families who work the land carefully.

▼ *Not a car in sight!* Most people in Beijing (Peking), the Chinese capital, travel to work by bus or by bicycle. So there is less pollution from rush-hour traffic than in the cities of Western Europe, the USA or Japan. In fact, the air pollution **per person** from China is less than from the richer countries of the world. China has more than 30 cities with over a million people.

A BEAUTIFUL SCENE?

Look more carefully! Forests are destroyed and a mountain is blasted away for a big project in China. It all looks lovely on this painting – but what about the environment?

JAPAN (Nippon) has many beautiful flowers. Most of Japan is mountainous and unspoilt. But pollution is a big problem in the crowded lowland areas, as the foreground of this photograph of Mt. Fuji shows. Japan imports vast amounts of coal and oil to power its many successful industries. The government allows whaling and hunting for dolphins, and permits the import of ivory from elephant tusks. The building industry in Japan also uses lots of tropical hardwoods from the world's rain forests.

East Asia stretches from high cold Tibet to the hot rice-growing lands near the South China Sea. North Korea and South Korea are two separate countries. Mongolia has fewer people for its area than any other country in the whole world – even though it is next to China, which has more people than any other country.

China has more than 1,226,000,000 people, so the future China is a very important environmental question. The west of China is not crowded, and some of the deserts and mountains are as empty as Mongolia. But the lowlands of eastern China are very crowded indeed. In fact, one in five of ALL the world's people live in eastern China. Chinese industry is now growing fast. It is based on low wages.

BERRY BUSHES OF EAST ASIA

If you've got a bush with bright winter berries in your garden or on the grounds of your school, it is probably of East Asian origin. Bushes like cotoneaster and pyrocanthus are developed from plants first grown there. These berries help birds to survive in winter – so you are helping the garden birds, and if you're lucky some wild birds will fly in for a feast when all the berries in the hedgerows have been eaten.

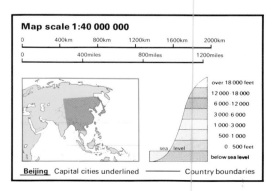

Map scale 1:40 000 000

| 0 | 400km | 800km | 1200km | 1600km | 2000km |

| 0 | 400miles | 800miles | 1200miles |

over 18 000 feet
12 000 - 18 000
6 000 - 12 000
3 000 - 6 000
1 000 - 3 000
500 - 1 000
0 - 500 feet
below sea level

Beijing Capital cities underlined ——— Country boundaries

Southeast Asia

▲ **Cooling off** in a swamp on Sulawesi, Indonesia. Sulawesi is the "H"-shaped island east of Borneo — a remote mountainous home to many rare species of plants, birds and animals, including this anoa.

◀ **Rice terraces** in the Philippines. The steep hillside has been carved by hand into flat terraces, which can be flooded to the right depth. The farmers and their families live in the little village, halfway up the hillside on the right. In the background an even steeper hillside is still covered with natural rain forest.

Rice is the world's most important grain, because it feeds far more people than any other crop. While the much bigger nations of China and India grow more, five countries in Southeast Asia (Indonesia, Thailand, Vietnam, Burma and the Philippines) are among the world's "top ten" producers of rice.

▶ **A rice plant** ready for harvesting is shown on this stamp from Sabah, a state in north Borneo that is part of the Federation of Malaysia. Several harvests of the crop can be grown each year in this part of the world.

THE RICE CYCLE

1. Preparing the land...
... is hard work in the flooded paddy fields. Some farmers now use rotovators, but this is still far too expensive for most ordinary families.

2. Planting...
... is tiring, back-breaking and wet work. The young seedlings are transplanted from the "nursery" into the flooded fields. This work is all done by hand.

3. Growing...
... is the only easy part! Plentiful water and hot sunshine result in quick growth, with some areas managing to produce three crops every year.

4. Harvesting...
... is done in dried-out fields. Again, it's very hard work. Some farmers now have two-wheeled gasoline-driven harvesters, but for most families the techniques they use throughout the cycle are the same ones used for hundreds of years in Southeast Asia.

▲ **Tin mining** in Malaysia. This was a tin-mining area. The rain forest has been destroyed and rivers in the area are still poisoned.

DEVELOPMENT . . . . . ?
. . . . . OR DEVASTATION?

Tin mining in Malaysia helped to bring "development": railroads, roads and jobs. Malaysia is the world's biggest producer of tin. The mineral is washed out of the ground by fierce jets of water. But tin is a "robber economy": once the tin has gone there is only waste land left.

Malaysia also exports natural rubber and palm oil, but these "primary products" are no longer the main exports. Proton cars and electronic goods are the "growth" industries today – along with tourism.

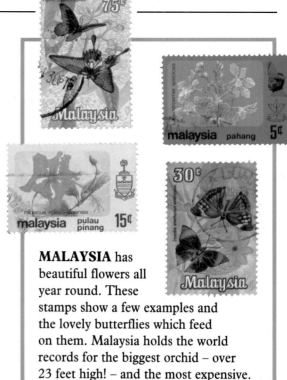

MALAYSIA has beautiful flowers all year round. These stamps show a few examples and the lovely butterflies which feed on them. Malaysia holds the world records for the biggest orchid – over 23 feet high! – and the most expensive. To trade in them is illegal.

◄ **Singapore** is the world's most crowded major independent country, with 12,510 people per square mile, and is famous for its amazing modern skyscrapers (in the background). Yet Sentosa Island (in the foreground) has forests and a national park. The monorail (center) helps thousands of visitors to see the island without spoiling it.

▶ **To understand this map** it's helpful to look at some other pages. The map on page 22 shows that some islands, such as Java and Bali, are very crowded, but other parts of Southeast Asia have few people. Page 40 shows that Indonesia and the Philippines are made up of lots of islands, while Malaysia is mainland plus parts of the island of Borneo. Page 41 shows that almost all of Southeast Asia was once forested, but the forests are now being felled at a frightening rate.

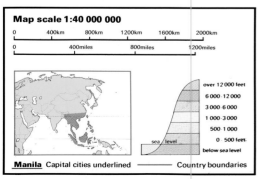

Map scale 1:40 000 000

| 0 | 400km | 800km | 1200km | 1600km | 2000km |

| 0 | 400miles | 800miles | 1200miles |

over 12 000 feet
6 000-12 000
3 000-6 000
1 000-3 000
500-1 000
0-500 feet
sea level
below sea level

Manila Capital cities underlined ——— Country boundaries

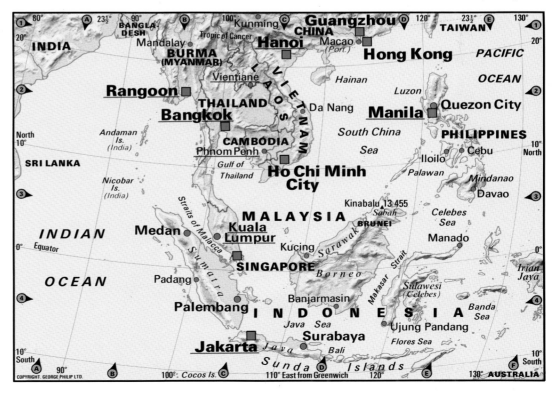

AFRICA

Africa is BIG! It is nearly 5,000 miles from east to west and from north to south. It's a continent with superb wildlife, especially in the savanna areas ("bush") where there is a mixture of grass and trees.

Much of Africa is desert and semidesert, not just in the north (everyone knows about the Sahara), but also in the east (called "the Horn of Africa" because of its shape) and in the southwest (including the Namib and the Kalahari). The savanna areas come between the deserts and the tropical forest. There is more desert than savanna, and more savanna than tropical forest.

Africa has more countries than any other continent. On a sea journey from Morocco to Cameroon you would pass 13! Some of them encourage conservation: they work to protect animals that are threatened by poaching, and set up national parks and wildlife reserves. Some areas have terrible droughts, famines or wars; the human inhabitants suffer badly, but the whole environment and its wildlife suffer too.

◄ *The "King of Beasts,"* pictured in Luanwa National Park, Zambia. The lion spends much of his time asleep. But when he's hungry he's very fierce – and, like his lionesses, he's a good hunter. Lions now enjoy protection in many areas of Africa.

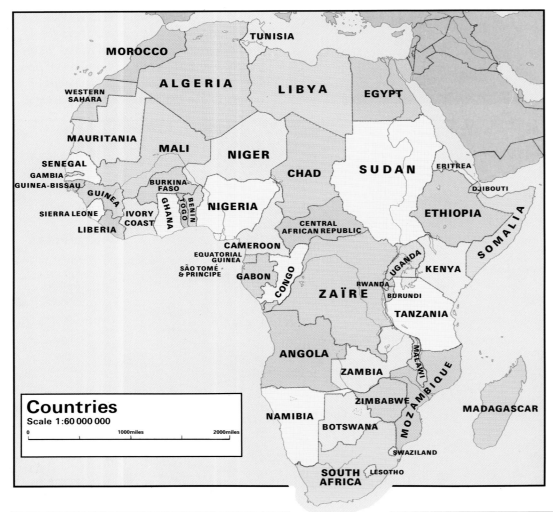

Countries

Scale 1:60 000 000

0   1000miles   2000miles

▲ **"Save the seashore birds":** a "Conservation Education" project run by the RSPB in Ghana.

▼ **Black storks** flying along the great Nile River – but which are the birds and which are their shadows? (Answer on page 96.)

(Answer on page 96.)

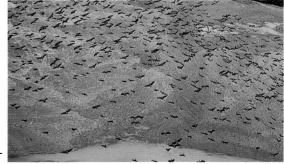

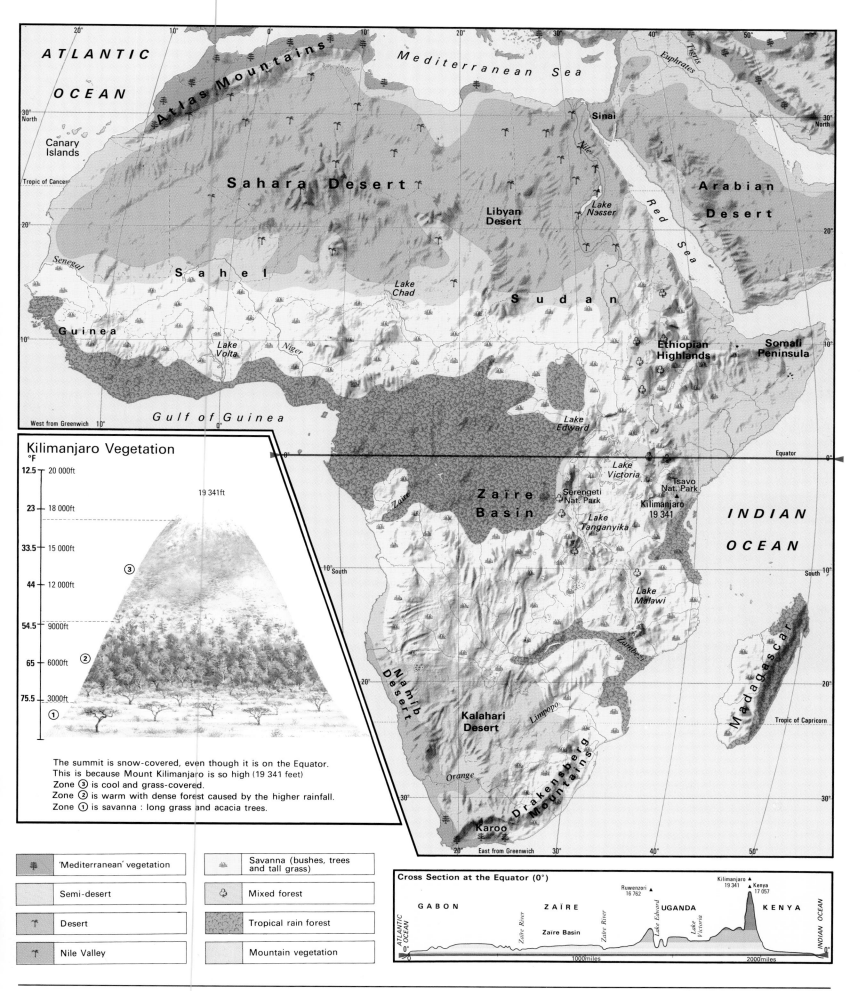

Kilimanjaro Vegetation

The summit is snow-covered, even though it is on the Equator.
This is because Mount Kilimanjaro is so high (19 341 feet)
Zone ③ is cool and grass-covered.
Zone ② is warm with dense forest caused by the higher rainfall.
Zone ① is savanna: long grass and acacia trees.

Legend:
- 'Mediterranean' vegetation
- Semi-desert
- Desert
- Nile Valley
- Savanna (bushes, trees and tall grass)
- Mixed forest
- Tropical rain forest
- Mountain vegetation

Cross Section at the Equator (0°)

Northern Africa

North Africa is mostly desert — the great Sahara. It stretches across nearly the whole width of the continent and is shared by 13 countries. It's the biggest desert in the world — and it's getting bigger, especially along the southern edge. The area of semi-desert here is called the Sahel — Arabic for "border." People try to stop the desert spreading by planting trees and digging wells, but for most it's a losing battle. As with many problems of the environment, there are no easy answers.

▲ **Sand dunes, Taghit, Algeria.** *These huge dunes will probably cover the tall date palms in a few years. It's a beautiful picture — but it's a very harsh place for people, animals and plants to live. Only a tenth of the Sahara Desert is really sand; most of it is gravel and rock.*

◀ **Giraffes in the Sahara?** *This rock drawing by Stone Age people is in the desert mountains of northern Niger. The image of giraffes is very accurate, so the artists would almost certainly have seen giraffes nearby — although the people may have migrated from further south. The evidence of the drawing suggests that the Sahara was much wetter then than it is today. Unfortunately it is still getting drier — and larger, invading areas to the south.*

▲ **The people** *of North Africa know that water is the key to life. The courtyard of the Great Mosque at Kairouan, Tunisia, looks like an empty place. But every drop of water which falls here is saved underneath the courtyard. The people believe that water is the gift of Allah (God). The "well" in the corner of the picture is very interesting. . .*

▼ **Crisis in the Sahel.** *These cattle in Niger are thirsty. The land is changing into desert. Drought and overgrazing have resulted in nothing growing in the foreground — and the soil will blow away. There is "desertification" in all the semidesert areas south of the Sahara.*

▼ **. . . for a thousand years** *buckets have been lowered into the water that's stored underground. Look what centuries of hauling ropes has done to the hard marble! If everyone was so careful to conserve water, would we have fewer problems?*

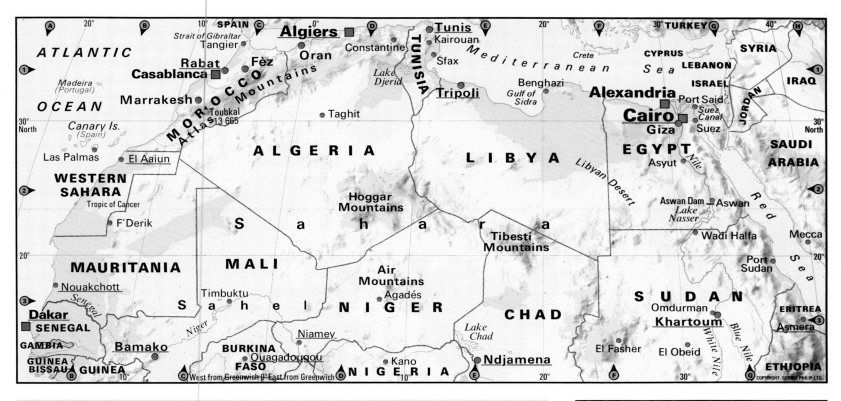

(map labels)
Strait of Gibraltar · Tangier
ATLANTIC
Algiers · Constantine
Tunis
Kairouan
SYRIA
Rabat · Fèz · Oran · Sfax
Crete
CYPRUS
LEBANON
Casablanca
TUNISIA
Mediterranean Sea
ISRAEL
IRAQ
Madeira (Portugal)
MOROCCO
Tripoli
Benghazi
Gulf of Sidra
Alexandria
Port Said
Suez Canal
OCEAN
Marrakesh
Lake Djerid
Cairo
Giza
Suez
JORDAN
30° North
Canary Is. (Spain)
Toubkal 13 665
Taghit
ALGERIA
LIBYA
Libyan Desert
EGYPT
Asyut
Nile
30° North
SAUDI ARABIA
Las Palmas
El Aaiun
Aswan Dam · Aswan
Lake Nasser
Red Sea
WESTERN SAHARA
Tropic of Cancer
Hoggar Mountains
Wadi Halfa
Mecca
20°
F'Derik
Sahara
Tibesti Mountains
Port Sudan
20°
MAURITANIA
MALI
Air Mountains
Agadés
SUDAN
Nouakchott
Timbuktu
Sahel
NIGER
CHAD
Omdurman
Khartoum
ERITREA
Asmera
Senegal
Dakar
SENEGAL
Niger
Niamey
Lake Chad
White Nile
Blue Nile
GAMBIA
Bamako
BURKINA FASO
Ouagadougou
Kano
Ndjamena
El Fasher
El Obeid
GUINEA BISSAU
GUINEA
Ouagadougou
NIGERIA
ETHIOPIA
West from Greenwich 0° East from Greenwich
10° 0° 10° 20° 30°
COPYRIGHT GEORGE PHILIP LTD.

THE ASWAN HIGH DAM: For and against a huge development

Damming the Nile River at Aswan was a great idea – in theory. The good news is printed in normal type, but the *italic type* gives a different story:

- Lots of electricity from hydroelectric power – *but most people can't afford it.*
- Power forever – *but Lake Nasser is filling up with silt, and it may last only a hundred years.*
- No more floods in Egypt – *but the silt from the yearly floods made the soil fertile, and now it's less fertile than it was before.*
- More water for people near the dam, and lots of fish to catch – *but 40,000 Nubian people lost their homes and farmland, and the water causes more malaria and bilharzia, both killer diseases.*
- There are some other "buts," too: *Less Nile water reaches the delta, so salty seawater is seeping into the soils near the coast, and crops do not grow so well now. And the delta is now being eroded by the sea.* This massive scheme shows many of the problems of bringing modern engineering techniques into a stable environment. Was it really worth building the dam?

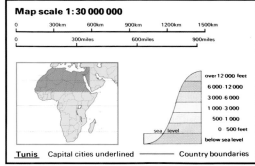

Map scale 1:30 000 000

0   300km   600km   900km   1200km   1500km
0   300miles   600miles   900miles

over 12 000 feet
6 000-12 000
3 000-6 000
1 000-3 000
500-1 000
0-500 feet
sea level
below sea level

Tunis   Capital cities underlined   ———— Country boundaries

▼ **"Egypt is the gift of the Nile."**
This satellite picture shows that Egypt is all dry, yellow-brown desert except where the water of the Nile River can be used for irrigation. The fertile Nile Valley and the triangular delta, the most crowded areas in Africa, are seen as dark blue.

◄ **The Aswan Dam** on the Nile in southern Egypt. You can see the power of the water (foreground), the electricity pylons (center) and the massive concrete dam itself (background). This was Egypt's largest construction project since the Pyramids, and was finished in 1964 with aid from the USSR. Water flows into Lake Nasser all year from wet areas far to the south.

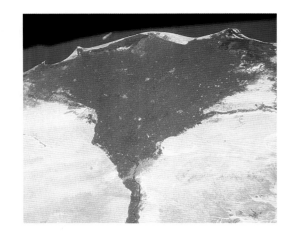

West and Central Africa

West and Central Africa are areas of great contrasts. There is spectacular rain forest, *but* much of it has been cleared (see below). People work hard growing lots of crops such as corn, cassava, groundnuts, cocoa, coffee, pineapples and bananas, *but* the prices they get are too low. There are new roads, *but* many of them cannot be used by vehicles after heavy rain. There is oil in Nigeria (Africa's biggest producer), *but* many countries have to import all their oil. And every country has a big international airport – *but* most ordinary people cannot afford to travel by air.

RIVER THAT FLOWS TWO WAYS!

The map opposite shows the Niger River flowing southward through Nigeria to the Niger delta (square C2). But did you know that the river flowing northeast through Guinea and Mali (square B1) is *also* the Niger River? Near Timbuctu (map page 55, square C3) this river changes direction.

Long ago there were two rivers. One river flowed north to an inland lake. The river that flowed to the coast "captured" it – and the lake vanished. But the old lake bed is an important wetland area for migrating birds, and an area of fertile soil.

THE DISAPPEARING LAKE

Lake Chad (map square D1) is a large "inland drainage basin" shared by Chad, Niger and Nigeria. To the south are the savanna lands. Rivers flow from here in the wet season, but vanish in the dry season. Less water flows into the lake than in the past because there is lower rainfall in some years – and because more water is being taken from the rivers for irrigation and for cattle. So Lake Chad is "shrinking."

WEST AFRICA'S TROPICAL RAIN FORESTS: A sad story . . .

▲ Even this stamp from Ghana shows a stump instead of a big tree. . . .

The scene from Gabon (right) explains the tale of destruction. Some of the huge trees are cut down to make bridges . . . so that more and bigger tree trunks can be taken away by giant trucks. Destroying the forest hasn't helped many people in these countries – most ordinary folk are still very poor. The wood has been used mainly for furniture and buildings in Europe, North America and Japan. What a waste – it will take centuries to grow to maturity again.

◀ *Children of the forest.* These children live near the Korup National Park in the Cameroons – one of the world's finest areas of tropical rain forest. There are lots and lots of children! You can see babies being carried on the backs of older sisters. When they grow up, will they cut down the forests for wood and for farmland? The answer would once have been "yes." But now WWF and the Cameroon government are trying to conserve the national park and to find other ways for these villagers to make a living. Tourism is one good idea . . . and better farming outside the national park is another. It's no good for conservationists just to say "no" and "stop"; they must find ways of preventing destruction while still giving the local people a decent living. Banana palms can be seen growing behind the children.

▼ **The map shows** the "heart of Africa": the forest lands and the savanna. Almost everywhere is very hot, except up in the mountains. It's a complicated map, with many varied countries, much poverty and lots of political problems – but there is some wonderful vegetation and wildlife too. Let's hope some of it can be conserved for future generations to enjoy.

NO IVORY IN THE "IVORY COAST"

The only ivory you're likely to see in West Africa nowadays is a picture, like this one on a matchbox! Millions of elephants have been killed for their ivory tusks, which were carved into piano keys, ornaments and chess sets. The country called "Ivory Coast" (Côte-d'Ivoire is the official French title) is still named after this cruel trade. But turn the page – there are lots of elephants. . . .

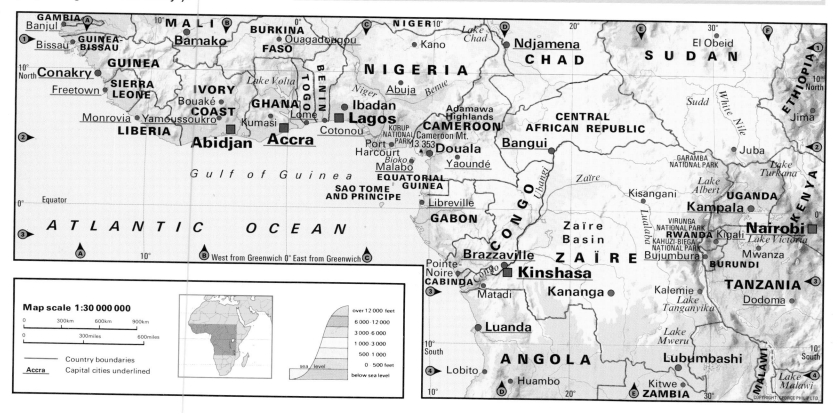

Map scale 1:30 000 000

| 0 | 300km | 600km | 900km |

| 0 | 300miles | 600miles |

— Country boundaries
Accra Capital cities underlined

over 12 000 feet
6 000-12 000
3 000-6 000
1 000-3 000
500-1 000
0-500 feet
sea level
below sea level

NATIONAL PARKS IN ZAÏRE:
A good idea . . .

PARC NATIONAL DE KAHUZI-BIEGA
Institut Zairois pour la Conservation de la Nature

▲ **A very rare car sticker.**
Can you translate the words?
(Answer on page 96.)

Gorillas are an endangered species, and Zaïre* needs money to conserve them. But Zaïre is a very poor country. So the solution is to charge foreign tourists a very high fee to visit the animals – 100 US dollars. Local people can visit for much less money. The result is that there is money for conservation and the number of visitors is controlled. The local people now have a good reason for preserving the forest.

The mountain gorilla is the world's largest primate. It is mainly vegetarian and consumes vast amounts of fruit, leaves and shoots. It lives only in the upland tropical forests of Zaïre, Rwanda and Uganda. They are killed for meat, hides and trophies, but the main threat to their future is the destruction of their habitat, made worse by civil war in the 1990s.

▶ **A hippopotamus** in Virunga National Park, Zaïre. Could this amazing animal own the biggest mouth in the world?

▼ **Lions** in Garamba National Park, Zaïre.

15z ZAÏRE
PARC DE LA GARAMBA — LIONS

8z ZAÏRE
PARC DES VIRUNGA — Hippopotames

* At the time of going to press, the government of Zaïre had been overthrown by rebels who planned to rename the country "The Democratic Republic of the Congo."

East Africa

▲ **Elephants in Ngorongoro Crater, Tanzania.** *The African elephant is the world's biggest land animal, and some in this herd weigh six tons! Their ears are bigger than you are! Herds travel many miles in a day, eating grass and tree bark — but they don't kill any animals for food. Yet man has killed vast numbers of elephants for the ivory in their tusks. Nearly a million elephants were killed in the 1980s. In Tanzania and Kenya game wardens fight the poachers, and the Kenyan government burns any ivory it takes from them.*

▼ **Zebras in the Masai Mara game reserve, Kenya.** *Look carefully: how many are there? Everyone says that zebras have no camouflage, but the baby seems to be well hidden. Nobody knows why zebras have stripes like this — or why different zebras have different patterns. We do know that animals like lions only see in black and white, so the stripes may act as camouflage to them. You can see forest in the background of the picture — this is a river valley where the extra water means more trees can grow.*

East Africa is *the* place to go to see "wild" wildlife. The money that tourists spend helps to conserve the herds of animals: not just the famous ones like elephants, giraffes and zebra, but also warthogs and many species of antelope too. There are far too many species to show them all on these pages or even in a book this size. Several of the important ones now enjoy protection on nature reserves run by governments.

Most of East Africa is highland, but the huge rift valleys are much lower, with many lakes where fantastic birds are seen.

In these parts of Africa, the population is rising fast. So there are sometimes conflicts between the needs of people and the needs of animals. After all, it must be very annoying if an elephant walks over your vegetable patch. . . .

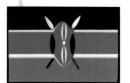

THE FLAG OF KENYA has a Masai warrior's shield and two spears – the defense of freedom. Black stands for the African people; red represents the blood of *all* people; green is for the fertile land of Kenya.

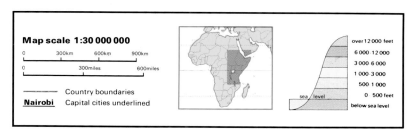

Map scale 1:30 000 000

| 0 | 300km | 600km | 900km |
| 0 | 300miles | 600miles |

—————— Country boundaries
Nairobi Capital cities underlined

over 12 000 feet
6 000–12 000
3 000–6 000
1 000–3 000
500–1 000
0–500 feet
below sea level
sea level

▲ *A water hole in the Serengeti National Park, Tanzania.*
It's not only humans who damage landscapes: you can see that these animals have destroyed the vegetation near the water. This is a photograph taken in the dry season – the bushes would be green in the wet season. The national parks of East Africa are among the best in the world. There are strict rules, such as no shooting (except with cameras!) and no feeding of the animals. In many places, you must not get out of your car because it's too dangerous.

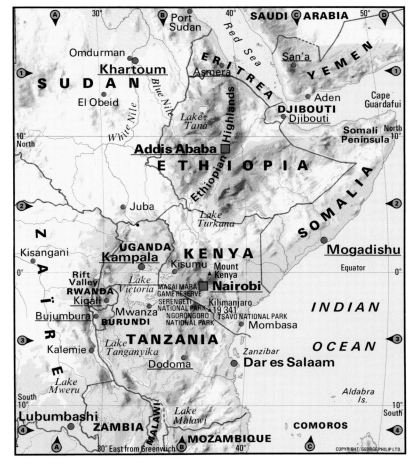

UGANDA & RWANDA

The landlocked countries of Uganda and Rwanda have suffered terribly from civil wars, but these beautiful birds have survived, and so have the bright flowers. The "crowned crane" is the national emblem of Uganda. Rwanda's civil war of 1994 led to at least a million deaths and millions of refugees – and harmed the environment too (see page 14).

DID YOU KNOW?

• Nairobi, the Kenyan capital, has more skyscrapers than many European cities.
• Northern Kenya is desert, not savanna.
• The population of Kenya has doubled in just 20 years (see page 23).
• There is snow on Mt. Kenya and Mt. Kilimanjaro, even though they are near the Equator (see page 53).
• The water of Lake Victoria flows northward along the Nile River for over 3,000 miles.

BEAUTIFUL OCEAN

East Africa has a coastline on the Indian Ocean. The water is warm, with lots of amazing fish. The stamp shows a "butterfly" fish in the coral. Now this is threatened by pollution and tourists. Coral is easily damaged and needs protection. Other coral areas have similar problems (see page 83).

Southern Africa

▶ **The white rhinoceros** is a very rare animal. There are five species of rhino, all of them near extinction. They are hunted by poachers for their horn, which sells for ridiculous prices on the "black market." It is smuggled to eastern Asia (for use in traditional medicines) and to the Yemen in the Middle East (for carving into dagger handles). The worst affected species is the northern square-lipped white rhino: there are just 25 of them left in the wild.

Trade in rhino horn is now banned – and there's some more good news, too. The white rhino of southern Africa is increasing in number: 100 years ago it had almost died out, but now there are over 5,000, because of careful conservation. However, the white rhinos of Zaïre are still at risk and so are the black rhinos of southern Africa. Rhinos are also found in southern parts of Asia – and they are rare and endangered there, too.

▶ **Lesotho** is a small, very poor country in southern Africa, previously called Basutoland. It is completely surrounded by South Africa. The stamp shows the red-headed finch (male and female).

◀ **Ostriches** do NOT put their "head in the sand" when they want to avoid a problem. The ostriches in this picture are kindly putting their heads in view for us! Perhaps it's human beings who have "heads in the sand"... about the need to conserve the environment. Ostriches were once bred for big feathers for women's hats. Now this useless trade has ended, we can again admire the world's biggest bird. Its eggs are so large they take half an hour to cook! Ostriches may not be able to fly, but they can run at amazing speeds....

CHAMELEONS can change color, to blend with the color of their surroundings. This chameleon is green, to match the leaves. It lives in Réunion, an Indian Ocean island that is still ruled by France – so it's on a French stamp with a French slogan we can all understand: *"Protection de la Nature."*

PLANTS OF SOUTH AFRICA
Many South African plants are different from anywhere else in the world. The "cycad" (left) is one of the oldest that exist: it's like a dinosaur of the plant world! Fossils like the cycad are found in rocks that are millions of years old. It looks rather like a date palm, and is protected in some countries by law. If you grow "red-hot pokers" in your garden, you already know one South African plant. This photograph (right) shows wild aloes – a close relative of the red-hot poker.

MADAGASCAR has been an island for 50 million years, and now it has many animals and plants that can be found only on this island. Over 5,000 plants or trees are unique to Madagascar. Some of them are related to plants in Australia – evidence that, long ago, Madagascar was joined to Australia. So Madagascar is a very special and very important island for everyone interested in conservation and in the world's different environments.

Did you know? The "rosy periwinkle" plant of Madagascar helps to save the lives of many children who have cancer. That's one more reason for conserving the natural world!

▶ **The black lemur** of Madagascar is a shy, tree-living mammal that wakes up at night. There are 19 subspecies of lemur in Madagascar – but they are threatened by the cutting down of the rain forest in which they live.

"DEAD AS A DODO"

The dodo was a flightless bird that lived only on the island of Mauritius, in the Indian Ocean. The dodo had no enemies, and lived happily until Portuguese sailors first saw them in 1507. People then hunted them without mercy and by 1681 they had become extinct. The phrase "dead as a dodo" means "completely extinct." Today, many other species are threatened – including the beautiful cheetah, the fastest runner in the world. But even the world's fastest animal is not safe from poachers with powerful and accurate hunting rifles. We must stop this and other species becoming as "dead as a dodo."

◀ **This picture** of a dodo was painted in the 1620s, before the strange creature became extinct.

▼ **A cheetah** on a stamp from Zimbabwe, a country with many exciting wild animals.

SOUTHERN AFRICA is one of the world's best places for wildlife: elephants, giraffes, zebras, and many different types of antelopes. It also has unusual vegetation (see opposite page). But there are problems too. Civil wars in Angola and Mozambique raged for years. And the environment, as well as the people, suffers from war.

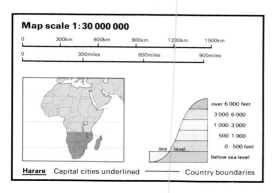

Map scale 1:30 000 000

| 0 | 300km | 600km | 900km | 1200km | 1500km |
| 0 | | 300miles | 600miles | | 900miles |

over 6 000 feet
3 000–6 000
1 000–3 000
500–1 000
0–500 feet
sea level
below sea level

<u>Harare</u> Capital cities underlined ——— Country boundaries

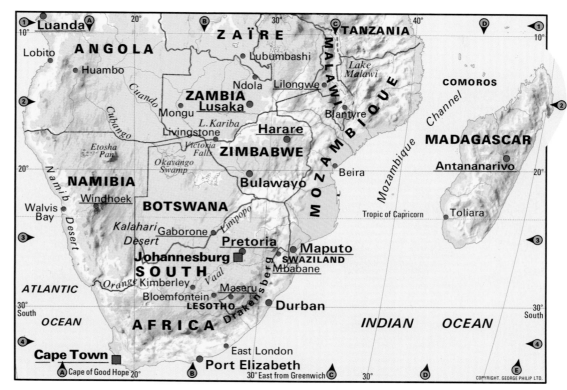

NORTH AMERICA

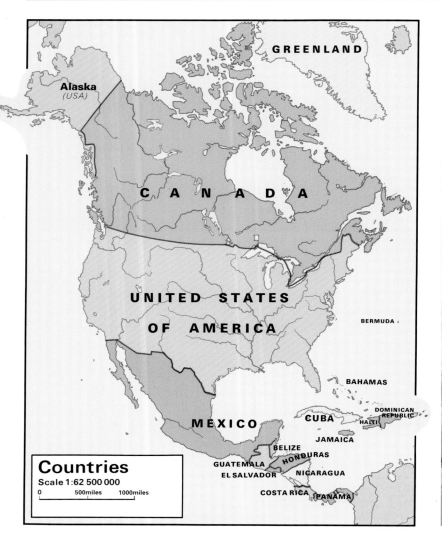

Countries
Scale 1:62 500 000

0   500miles   1000miles

Think of North America and you probably think of a comfortable life in a temperate climate. But that's only right for a small part of the continent. Most of it is not temperate at all. The vast northern lands of Alaska and northern Canada have long and bitterly cold winters. Central America, by contrast, is mostly tropical. Parts of Mexico are desert or semidesert, but the seven smaller countries are hot and wet, originally with superb rain forests.

The eight countries of Central America link North and South America at present – but for many millions of years there was a big gap, and the two continents have very different animals and plants as well as sharing the more common ones.

▲ **This walrus** in the Bering Strait, between North America and Asia, doesn't mind the cold. The Bering Strait freezes in winter – so there is a "bridge" between the two continents. For many millions of years, America and Asia were joined here. That's why many of the land animals on these two continents are so similar. The walrus is still hunted for its blubber and ivory tusks.

◄ **Bison** in Yellowstone National Park, Wyoming, USA. There were once 60 million bison on the Great Plains of North America, and they were essential to the lives of the Indians. But they were hunted by the white men in the last century – in the 1870s over two million were killed every year. Only a few survived, but now they're protected, and numbers have reached 50,000.

▲ Cones and needles of the white pine, on a Canadian stamp. The map shows that large areas of southern Canada have coniferous forests. The USA and Canada are the first and third biggest producers of paper, and Canada is by far the world's biggest exporter.

	Tundra : mosses, lichens and dwarf trees
	Rainforest
♧	Temperate forest (broad-leaved trees)
♣	Temperate forest (coniferous trees)
♯	'Mediterranean' vegetation
ᴧᴧᴧ	Temperate grassland and savanna
	Semi-desert (thorn bushes and cacti)
ⵣ	Desert

▼ A tropical landscape in Central America. The tall trees are coconut palms, with a mango tree growing behind the nearest one. The green-and-yellow tree is a banana palm. In the foreground is dasheen, a root crop that likes the hot, wet climate.

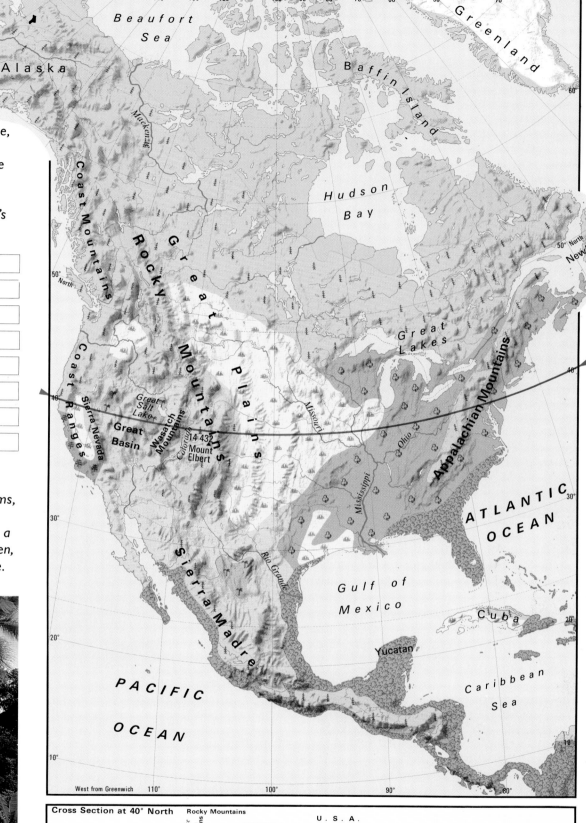

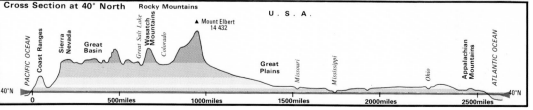

Cross Section at 40° North

63

Canada

Canada is one of the least crowded countries in the world – there are fewer than eight people per square mile (by comparison, Belgium, the Netherlands and Japan each have over 765 people per square mile). So there really is space for nature as well as for farmland and cities in Canada – and there are far fewer environmental problems than in most other countries.

Canadians are proud of their varied and beautiful landscapes, as the coats of arms of some provinces show (below right). Most Canadians live in the southern parts of their huge country, which is the world's second biggest. Did you realize that the largest city, Toronto, is nearer to the Equator than it is to the North Pole, and further south than Milan in sunny Italy?

▼ *The "tundra" is the name given to the northern lowlands of Canada. It is a vast area. Snow covers the ground in the long winter, but there are bright colors in the short summer – reds, greens and browns. There are no trees, because the subsoil is always frozen and the roots of trees cannot survive. Few people live here – but to the moose, it's the best place on Earth! (See 25-cent coin below.)*
★ There's more about the tundra on page 87 – "The Arctic" ★

▲ **The Rocky Mountains in summer.** *The landscape was shaped by ice. This photograph was taken in Banff National Park. Tourists bring money in, and so help to conserve the national parks.*

▼ **A hard-working beaver** *brings another piece to repair his dam. Inside the dam is a "lodge" for the family. The only entrance is below the water, which helps keep the family safe. You can see another beaver on the 5-cent coin below.*

▶ **The leaves of the maple** *turn bright red in the autumn. This is Canada's national tree, and a maple leaf is featured on its flag.*

ANIMALS ON COINS: a beaver (5 cents) and a moose (25 cents). The antlers of a fully grown male moose can grow up to an impressive span of seven feet across.

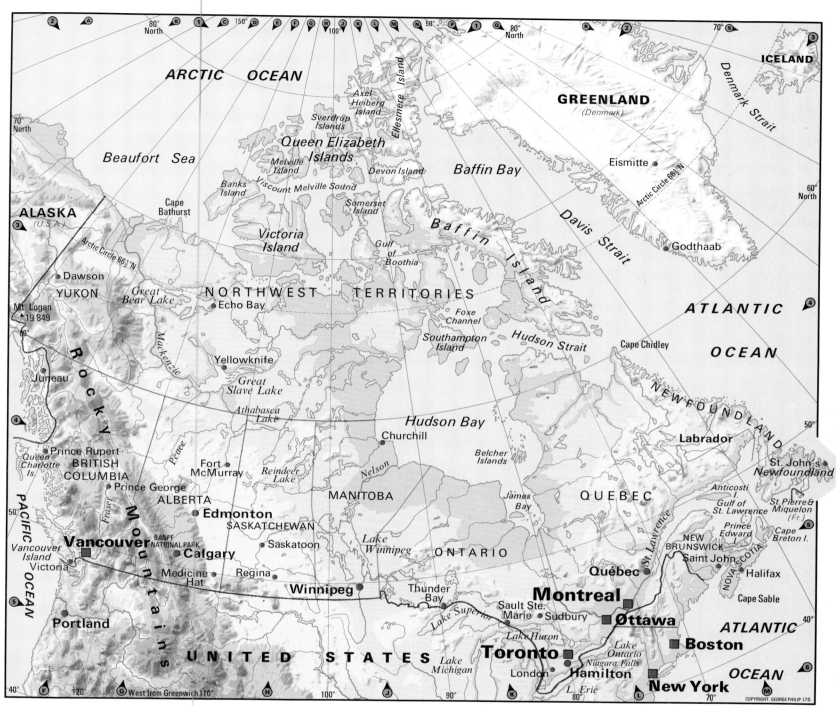

ARCTIC OCEAN

ICELAND

GREENLAND
(Denmark)

Beaufort Sea

Axel
Heiberg
Island

Sverdrup
Islands

Queen Elizabeth
Islands

Denmark Strait

Melville
Island

Devon Island

Baffin Bay

Eismitte

Banks
Island

Viscount Melville Sound

Somerset
Island

Arctic Circle 66½°N

Cape
Bathurst

ALASKA
(U.S.A.)

Victoria
Island

Gulf
of
Boothia

Baffin Island

Davis Strait

60°
North

Godthaab

70°
North

Arctic Circle 66½°N

Dawson

YUKON

Great
Bear Lake

N O R T H W E S T   T E R R I T O R I E S

Echo Bay

Foxe
Channel

ATLANTIC

OCEAN

Cape Chidley

70°

Mt. Logan
▲19,849

Juneau

Mackenzie

Yellowknife

Great
Slave Lake

Southampton
Island

Hudson Strait

60°

Athabasca
Lake

Hudson Bay

NEWFOUNDLAND

50°

Churchill

Labrador

Queen
Charlotte
Is.

Prince Rupert

BRITISH
COLUMBIA

Peace

Fort
McMurray

Reindeer
Lake

Nelson

Belcher
Islands

St. John's
Newfoundland

Prince George

ALBERTA

MANITOBA

James
Bay

QUEBEC

Anticosti
I.
Gulf of
St. Lawrence

St. Pierre &
Miquelon
(Fr.)

Edmonton

SASKATCHEWAN

Cape
Breton I.

50°

Vancouver

BANFF
NATIONAL PARK

Saskatoon

Lake
Winnipeg

ONTARIO

St. Lawrence

NEW
BRUNSWICK

Prince
Edward
I.

Vancouver
Island

Calgary

Medicine
Hat

Regina

Winnipeg

Thunder
Bay

Saint John

NOVA SCOTIA

Halifax

Victoria

Québec

Cape Sable

PACIFIC

OCEAN

Montreal

Sault Ste.
Marie

Sudbury

Ottawa

ATLANTIC

40°

Portland

Lake Superior

Toronto

Lake
Huron

Lake
Ontario

Niagara Falls

Hamilton

Boston

U N I T E D   S T A T E S

Lake
Michigan

London

L. Erie

New York

OCEAN

40°

West from Greenwich 110°

120°

100°

90°

80°

70°

COPYRIGHT. GEORGE PHILIP LTD.

COATS OF ARMS

◀ **Alberta's** coat of arms
shows the prairies in the
foreground, with the ripe
golden corn that dominates the
"wheat belt" of Canada. The
spectacular Rocky Mountains
can be seen in the background.

▶**Manitoba** is a central "prairie
province" of Canada and the
coat of arms shows a bison.

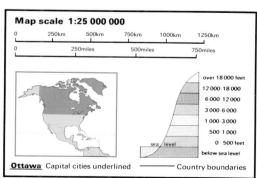

Map scale 1:25 000 000

| 0 | 250km | 500km | 750km | 1000km | 1250km |

| 0 | 250miles | 500miles | 750miles |

over 18 000 feet
12 000-18 000
6 000-12 000
3 000-6 000
1 000-3 000
500-1 000
0 - 500 feet
sea level
below sea level

Ottawa Capital cities underlined

Country boundaries

"BASMOQN": A "non-word" to help you
remember the big provinces (see page 96).

United States: 1

Imagine going on a car journey across the USA, west from New York. It will take several days, but you'll soon reach the forested Appalachian Mountain ridges. It's a beautiful area, but there are scars of old coal mines as well. After that, you'll travel fast through the flat farmland of the Midwest, and cross the wide Mississippi near St. Louis. As you travel on, there's less rainfall and the grass looks dry. Then the landscape changes: there's a steep climb up the Rockies. You then travel through mountain and even desert before you reach the Sierra Nevada ("Snowy Mountains") and go downhill to the Central Valley of California and the Pacific coast near San Francisco.

◀ **The American eagle** is featured on the United States quarter-dollar coin. To the Indians, the bald eagle was a symbol of freedom. But white people hunted it and numbers fell drastically. Many of the eagles that survived then died from pesticides used in farming. Now with conservation programs, the number of eagles is growing again.

BLOWING HOT AND COLD

In offices in New York, people work in shirtsleeves in the cold winters – yet they sometimes need pullovers in the hot summer! Americans use enormous amounts of energy for heating offices in winter – and even more for air-conditioning them in summer.

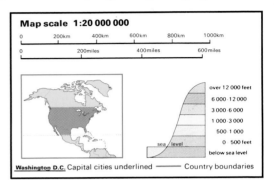

Map scale 1:20 000 000

| 0 | 200km | 400km | 600km | 800km | 1000km |

| 0 | 200miles | 400miles | 600miles |

over 12 000 feet
6 000 -12 000
3 000 -6 000
1 000 -3 000
500 -1 000
0 -500 feet
sea level
below sea level

Washington D.C. Capital cities underlined — Country boundaries

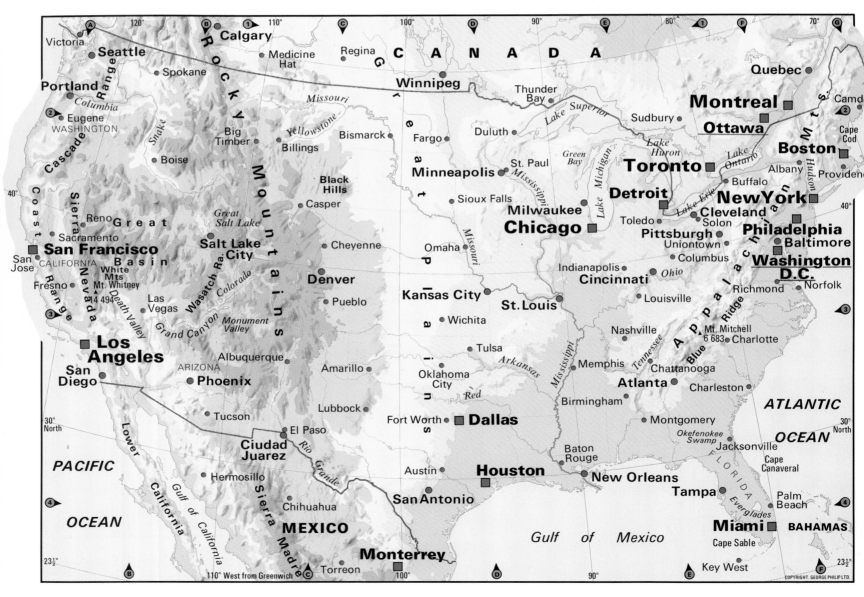

THE GOOD NEWS...

The USA is a big, mostly beautiful, and wonderfully varied country – as these lines from the patriotic song *America* show:

"O beautiful for spacious skies,
For amber waves of grain,
For purple mountain majesties
Above the fruited plain!"
[Katherine Lee Bates (1859–1929)]

▼ *The fall* in Camden, a small harbor town in Maine, the USA's most eastern state. This is when the broadleafed trees become a fiery red color. It's a picture of harmony between people and nature. There's certainly plenty of room for both: on average, each American has 16 times more space than every English person.

... AND THE BAD NEWS

▲ *Filthy water* pours out from a Pennsylvania steelworks into the river – and the name of the steelworks is displayed so boldly! Nobody seemed to care in 1968, when this picture was taken. This factory ruined the air as well as the water. Since then, the American anti-pollution laws have become more strict, and they are obeyed more – but there are still many pollution problems in many parts of the USA.

▼ *Pollution over New York.* It's a lovely day – with a clear blue sky – but not in America's biggest city. The exhausts from millions of cars have created SMOG (SMoke and fOG). Some people will die from it. Wouldn't it be better to ban cars from cities, and improve bus, train and subway services?

CONSERVATION ON STAMPS

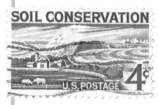

These three stamps were some of the first conservation ones ever to be printed. They were designed to encourage people to care for the environment. One stamp was issued each year from 1958 to 1961 (there was a forest conservation one as well). In those days, far fewer people were concerned about the environment.

▲ **Soil conservation.** The land (right) has been "contour plowed" to prevent gullies forming (see page 46).

▶ **Water conservation.** Every raindrop is precious. The dam has been built to conserve water – to prevent erosion, to allow irrigation, and to supply a town with water.

◀ **Range conservation.** "The range" is the name for grasslands of the West, where it's too dry for crops to grow. If this land is overgrazed, the soil can blow away or be eroded by water after a storm. There are now fears that global warming caused by the Greenhouse Effect may lead to this area being affected by drought – and becoming a "dust bowl."

▼ **The map shows** how many days in an average year are free of frost. There are huge differences: the southern states are often called the "sunbelt." Subtropical crops like cotton, rice and peanuts can be grown here, and it's a popular area for vacations and retirement.

The northern states are sometimes unkindly called the "rustbelt": salt on the snowy roads in winter makes the cars rust more quickly. Many of the factories are old – and some look rather rusty. Winters in the north of the USA can be bitterly cold, as the picture below the map shows.

SOME ENVIRONMENTAL "RECORDS" HELD BY THE USA:

The largest living thing in the world is a giant sequoia tree named "General Sherman." It's in Sequoia National Park, California, and it weighs over 6,000 tons. It's 266 feet high – taller than a 20-story office building! If it were chopped down, it could make 5,000,000,000 matches! Yet it grew from a tiny seed that weighed just five milligrams.

The oldest tree in the world was in California, in the Sierra Nevada, until it was cut down in the 1960s. What a tragedy: the bristlecone pine had grown for nearly 5,000 years. The oldest living tree today is of the same species: it grows on the White Mountains, California, and is an amazing 4,600 years old.

The largest fungus was an edible mushroom found near Solon, Ohio. It weighed over 70 pounds (32 kg). And the largest tree fungus ever found came from the USA as well – from the west coast, in the state of Washington. It weighed 300 pounds (136 kg).

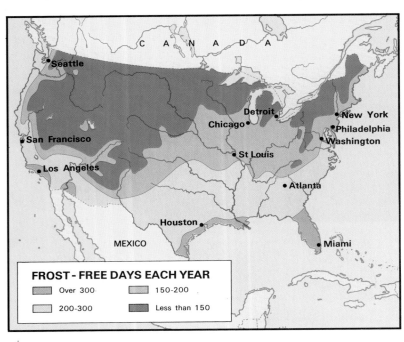

FROST - FREE DAYS EACH YEAR

Over 300	150-200
200-300	Less than 150

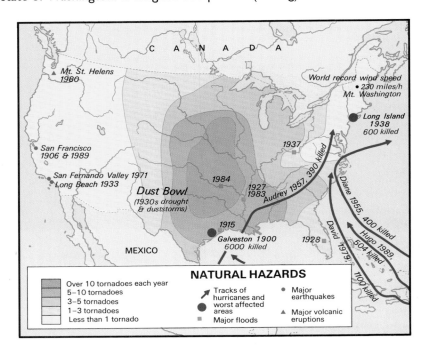

NATURAL HAZARDS

Over 10 tornadoes each year	
5–10 tornadoes	↗ Tracks of hurricanes and worst affected areas
3–5 tornadoes	● Major earthquakes
1–3 tornadoes	●
Less than 1 tornado	■ Major floods
	▲ Major volcanic eruptions

◄ **Destruction in the past ...**
A beautiful winter scene in the northern Appalachian Mountains – but all the trees except one are thin and weak. The big trees, which take centuries to grow, were almost all cut down for timber years ago.

► **... and conservation today.**
Dams on the Tennessee River are "multipurpose": they help stop soil erosion, improve navigation, and allow "clean" hydroelectric power to be generated. You can see a TVA (Tennessee Valley Authority) lake beyond the notice board. The lake has other uses too: it is popular for fishing, sailing and other water sports.

▲ **Hurricanes** are huge and tornadoes are tiny. But they both have very fast whirling winds, and they can cause terrible damage and death in many parts of the USA. The hurricanes start off the Caribbean Sea.

AMERICAN WILDERNESS

The six largest US National Parks are in Alaska, the biggest state. The largest is Wrangell-St. Elias, which joins on to a Canadian reserve. Alaska is shown at a smaller scale on the map (right).

► **National parks of the USA.**

The two main aims of these parks are conservation and appreciation of the landscape and wildlife. Visitors are encouraged to come, but there are careful controls. Some parks are crowded; others are almost empty. There are many state parks as well. The USA was the first country in the world to create national parks, and many countries have copied their example. The biggest on the main map is Yellowstone, the world's greatest area for geysers.

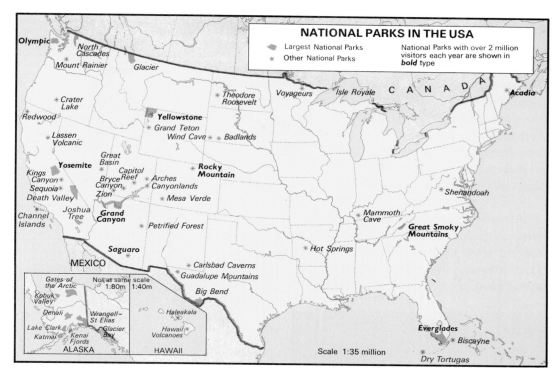

NATIONAL PARKS IN THE USA

Largest National Parks

* Other National Parks

National Parks with over 2 million visitors each year are shown in **bold** type

Olympic, North Cascades, Mount Rainier, Glacier, Crater Lake, Redwood, Lassen Volcanic, Theodore Roosevelt, Voyageurs, Isle Royale, CANADA, Acadia, **Yellowstone**, Grand Teton, Wind Cave, Badlands, Great Basin, Yosemite, Capitol Reef, Bryce Canyon, Kings Canyon, Sequoia, Zion, Death Valley, Arches, Canyonlands, **Rocky Mountain**, Mesa Verde, Shenandoah, Channel Islands, Joshua Tree, **Grand Canyon**, Petrified Forest, Mammoth Cave, **Great Smoky Mountains**, Saguaro, Hot Springs, MEXICO, Carlsbad Caverns, Guadalupe Mountains, Big Bend, **Everglades**, Biscayne, Dry Tortugas

Gates of the Arctic, Not at same scale 1:80m 1:40m, Kobuk Valley, Denali, Wrangell-St Elias, Haleakala, Lake Clark, Katmai, Kenai Fjords, Glacier Bay, Hawaii Volcanoes, ALASKA, HAWAII

Scale 1:35 million

◄ **Safe, dry land . . .**

This photograph of Arches National Park, Utah, has three contrasting elements: there is desert in the foreground, amazing arches caused by erosion in the middle ground, and snow-covered mountains in the background. There is plenty of space for visitors to this spectacular landscape.

▼ **. . . and threatened wetlands.**

The map below shows what might happen to Florida in the future, if the sea level rises because of the Greenhouse Effect. Whole cities such as Miami could almost vanish if the sea rose 26 feet. All of today's beautiful wetlands, including the Everglades National Park, would disappear – and much of the wetland wildlife would go too.

◄ **A bird's-eye view . . .**

In the Okefenokee Swamp, Florida, you can look down from a viewing tower and see a boat in the flooded forest.

► **. . . and a view of a bird!**

From the walkway you can see many birds, such as this beautiful egret. But if sea levels rise these wetlands will vanish, and with them wildlife that includes alligators and a large number of rare animals and plants.

GEORGIA, ATLANTIC OCEAN, Okefenokee Swamp, Jacksonville, Panama City, Daytona Beach, GULF OF MEXICO, Orlando, Disney World, Kennedy Space Center and Cape Canaveral, St. Petersburg, Tampa, Miami, Everglades National Park, Florida Keys

FLOODING IN FLORIDA

Land that would flood if the sea level rose by 13-26 feet

Swamps

Canals

0 50 100 150miles

A map of the American states in an "environment" atlas may seem surprising. But each government of the 50 states makes important decisions about the environment. They decide how strong their conservation rules will be, and they decide where state parks and state forests should be located.

Most states are very proud of their environment, and the flags and coats of arms or seals of some states show special features of their environment. For example, California has a handsome bear on its flag. Every US state has a state bird, a state flower and a state tree.

And no matter what the size of its population, each state sends two senators to the US Senate in Washington, DC – so each state can influence the laws on the environment that are passed there.

The two newest states – Alaska and Hawaii – are so different from the rest of the USA that they have a page of their own (opposite).

▼ *A moose crosses a river in the Denali National Park, Alaska . . . but her baby is too frightened to follow her through the fast, cold water. The youngster prefers the safety of the vast coniferous forest.*

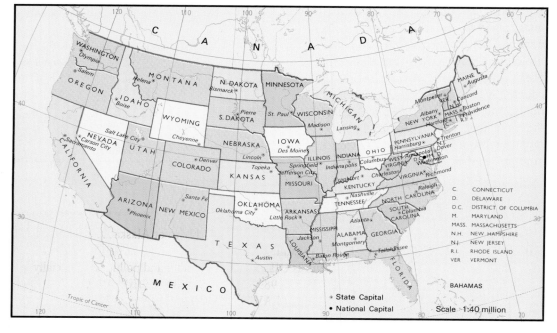

C.	CONNECTICUT
D.	DELAWARE
D.C.	DISTRICT OF COLUMBIA
M.	MARYLAND
MASS.	MASSACHUSETTS
N.H.	NEW HAMPSHIRE
N.J.	NEW JERSEY
R.I.	RHODE ISLAND
VER.	VERMONT

• State Capital
• National Capital

Scale 1:40 million

WHAT SOME STATE NAMES MEAN
Arizona: spring water (Indian);
Florida: flowers, **Montana:** mountainous,
Nevada: snow-capped (all Spanish);
Pennsylvania: Penn's woodland;
Vermont: green mountain (French).
Named after big rivers: Colorado, Delaware, Mississippi, Missouri, Ohio, Tennessee.

▼ **New York** has mountains in the north of the state. On the state seal we can see the Hudson River, with two sailing ships, and a mountain at sunset. The motto means "Ever upward." New York State stretches from the coast of the Atlantic Ocean north to the Great Lakes, which the United States shares with Canada.

▲ **Minnesota** has a seal showing a pioneer white farmer watching an Indian riding west; the white settlers are taking over his land.

◄ **Kansas** has a Midwest landscape at sunset on its state seal, with plowed land, pasture and distant hills.

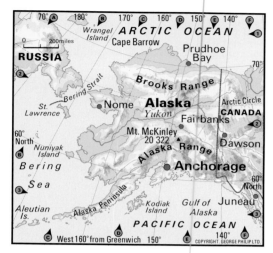

▶ **Mt. McKinley, Alaska.** *This is the highest mountain in the USA; the summit is 20,322 feet high. Fresh snow can fall even in summer. The snow is reflected in a lake in the tundra (foreground). The frozen subsoil makes the area marshy, and no trees can grow. This area is part of the huge Denali National Park, Alaska's third biggest.*

QUESTION: Why is thick, smelly, gooey black stuff a problem for Alaska...
...but the reason for the existence of Hawaii?
Alaska's thick, smelly, gooey black stuff is OIL. It brings wealth – and pollution, especially to the sea: 13 million gallons were spilled in 1989, much of it from the *Exxon Valdez*.
Hawaii's thick, smelly, gooey black stuff is LAVA – the islands are made of it (right).

CONTRASTS BETWEEN THE NEWEST STATES OF THE USA

Alaska ...
- Biggest state in the USA
- Most northerly state – and coldest
- Mostly mainland
- High mountains always snow-covered
- Mountains are mostly fold mountains
- Fewest people of any state
- Big oil developments threaten the small Inuit population and the environment
- State flower is *tiny* – a forget-me-not

Hawaii ...
- One of the smallest states
- Most southerly state – and warmest
- All islands
- High mountains never snow-covered
- Mountains are volcanoes
- Over a million people
- No oil – but beaches have some of world's biggest and best waves for surfing
- State flower is *big* – a yellow hibiscus

* Both states joined the Union in 1959, Alaska in January and Hawaii in August.

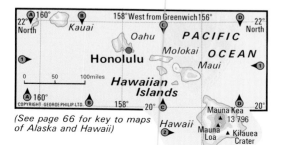

(See page 66 for key to maps of Alaska and Hawaii)

▶ **The islands of Hawaii** *are made from volcanic lava. Sometimes you can see new land being made! The hot lava even makes the seawater change into steam. This photograph was taken at Kilauea, on the biggest island, Hawaii. You can see how the red-hot molten lava soon cools to black lava, and makes ridges. (See also page 13.)*

Central America

There are eight countries in Central America. Mexico is much bigger than all the other seven countries put together and has over three-quarters of the total population of Central America – even though much of Mexico is very dry.

The other countries were once densely forested, but much of the forest has been cleared for farmland and banana plantations. Some of it, however, is still untouched. Even today there is no surfaced road and no railroad from North America to South America: the "Darien Gap" in eastern Panama is still a jungle barrier to travelers – and a joy to naturalists and conservationists of all kinds.

Which Central American country...
1 — has no coastline on the Pacific?
2 — has no coastline on the Caribbean?
3 — is partly outside the tropics?
4 — is the smallest? (two possible answers)
5 — has a famous canal connecting the Atlantic Ocean and the Pacific Ocean?
(Answers on page 96.)

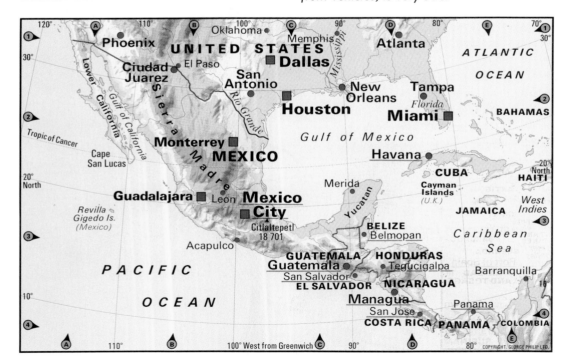

◀ *Giant cactus, Mexico.* Notice how dry the land looks – cacti can survive long droughts. The biggest cacti in the world are found here and in Arizona, USA. The Saguaro cactus can grow up to 52 feet – as high as a five-story apartment building.

▶ *Traffic jam in Mexico City.* The Mexican capital is one of the world's biggest cities. Shanty towns surround the city, and air pollution, especially from vehicles, is very bad.

▲ *It's not pollution!* Morning mist rises in Mexico, near the American border. This is a semidesert area, but springs of fresh water at the foot of the mountain allow people to live here. Many of them leave such areas to look for work in the USA.

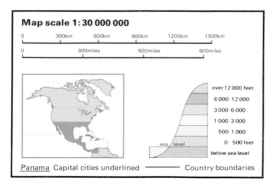

Map scale 1 : 30 000 000

Panama Capital cities underlined ———— Country boundaries

over 12 000 feet
6 000 - 12 000
3 000 - 6 000
1 000 - 3 000
500 - 1 000
0 - 500 feet
below sea level

The Caribbean

The Caribbean countries are a chain of beautiful islands – the tops of a mountain range that is mostly under the sea. There are varied environments, from high volcanoes with rich forests to low coral islands, some of which are quite dry. The photographs on this page come from the volcanic islands. There is no winter in this part of the world, and tourists visit all year.

Which Caribbean island...
1 — is the biggest?
2 — is the nearest one to the USA?
3 — is the nearest one to Honduras?
4 — is the nearest one to South America?
5 — belongs to the Netherlands?
6 — belongs to France?
7 — is shared by two countries?
(Answers on page 96.)

FLYING FISH don't fly – but they do jump out of the sea for a few seconds. And one of them "jumped" on to this seven-sided dollar coin from Barbados!

TWO RIVERS

Tourists enjoy visiting the rapids of Ocho Rios ("Eight Rivers") in Jamaica (left). But when a hurricane strikes, there can be floods. This concrete and steel bridge in Dominica (right) was destroyed.

▶ **A market stall** in Castries, capital of St Lucia. Palm trees are useful: they can be used for thatched roofs and also for hats, mats and baskets. Tourists will buy the goods, just as local families do. This is development that helps people while not harming the environment.

BANANAS are the main export from some of the Caribbean islands. This fine crop grows partly because of "poison" from the sky. A spray kills the bugs, but it can drift to the forest (background) and some of the poison will enter the rivers. Banana plants produce bunches of 100–200, which develop after 9 to 12 months – and go on producing for 5 to 20 years.

▼ **Mont Pelée,** a volcano on Martinique, is peaceful today. But in 1902 hot, poisonous gas came down the mountain from the crater and killed all 20,000 people (except one) in the former capital city of Saint-Pierre. Today, the forest is taking over – but the fine steps of the city hall can still be seen.

SOUTH AMERICA

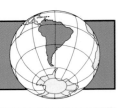

Countries

Scale 1:80 000 000

0   500miles   1000miles

South America can be seen as the world's biggest triangle. The western side of the "triangle" has the mighty Andes. The Andes are higher than any mountains in the world, apart from the mountains of central Asia. There is lots of snow and ice, and there are many volcanoes – though most of them are not active. In Bolivia there's a high plateau with South America's biggest lakes, including Lake Titicaca, shared with Peru.

* Which seven countries share the Andes?

The Amazon forest (most of which is in Brazil) occupies much of the east side of the "triangle" – but not all of it. Northeast Brazil has problems of drought, not of too much rain (see page 78). And parts of southern Brazil are savanna, not forest.

* There are 13 countries in South America, and Brazil touches all the others – except two. Can you see which two they are from the map above on the left?
(* Answers on page 96.)

▲ **The mighty Andes** seen from the air. The snow-covered peaks are in the sunshine above the clouds. The Andes are fold mountains, but these steep slopes have been carved by ice. This photograph was taken over Peru: it is a "high altitude" air photograph. The valleys are hidden below the cloud. The rivers there take the melted ice to the Atacama Desert on the west side of the Andes, and to rivers that flow for thousands of miles through the Amazon forest on the east side.

◄ **The Amazon rain forest** in Brazil is being destroyed at an alarming rate. The tall trees (top right) are being cut down. The big ones are sold; the rest are burned (right center). The new road (red strip on left) allows timber and crops to be moved out of the area. But the farmland (left) is not of good quality. The farmer who lives in the house to the left of the road is a poor man, and his family may wish they had not moved here. Other people moving into the rain forest include "prospectors" looking for gold – and the great mining companies searching for tin, manganese and bauxite (used for aluminum). This is a "low altitude" aerial photograph.

Legend

- Tropical rain forest
- Temperate forest
- Savanna and temperate grassland *
- Semi-desert (thorn bushes and scrub)
- Desert
- High mountain vegetation

* The map uses the same color for two different but similar environments. Outside the tropics, temperate grassland can be high, tough "pampas grass" or grazing land for cattle and sheep. Savanna is found in tropical areas that have a dry season; there are trees, bushes and thorny shrubs as well as long grass.

DID YOU KNOW that the mountains continue northward? The world map on page 6 shows that there are continuous mountains from South America, through Central and North America, all the way to Alaska. It's the world's longest mountain range. The Panama Canal cuts through one of the lowest points in the chain.

▼ *Natural rubber comes from trees that grow naturally in the Amazon rain forest. This man has collected rubber from inside the bark of the trees by making a cut in the bark. The rubber (latex) then drips out, and hardens in a few hours. But the collectors have an uncertain future because of:*
- *The cutting down of the forest.*
- *Rubber plantations in other countries.*
- *The development of "synthetic rubber" in chemical factories around the world.*

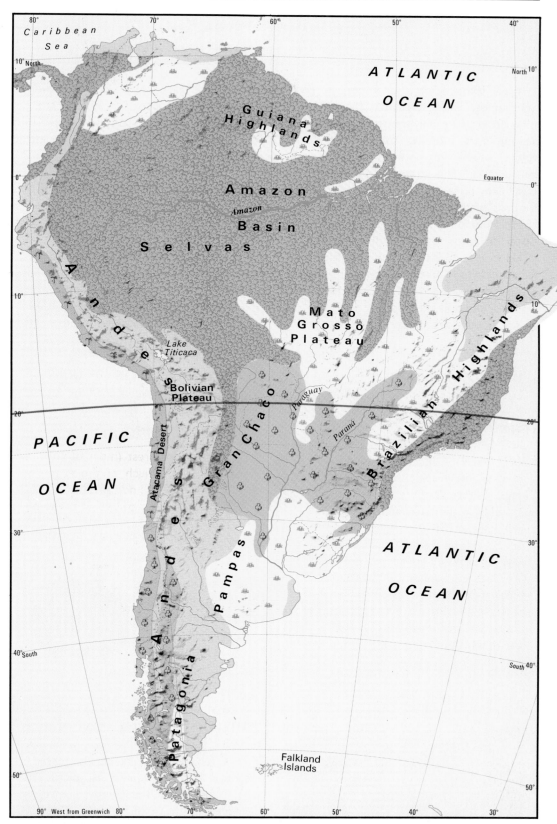

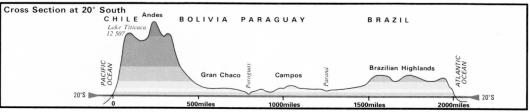

Cross Section at 20° South

CHILE BOLIVIA PARAGUAY BRAZIL

Andes
Lake Titicaca 12 507
PACIFIC OCEAN
Gran Chaco
Paraguay
Campos
Paraná
Brazilian Highlands
ATLANTIC OCEAN

20°S — 0 — 500miles — 1000miles — 1500miles — 2000miles — 20°S

The Andes

Imagine climbing up the Andes, in Peru. Start at the Pacific Ocean in the west and it's a desert. The only moisture comes from sea fog in the morning. You pass the shanty towns, where water shortages are a problem all year. The strata of the rock stand out, like bones on a skeleton. At the foothills of the Andes you find an "oasis" – rivers from the mountains provide enough water for crops to grow with irrigation.

Up in the Andes you find grassland, with llamas grazing. There's some nasty pollution around the mining town of Cerro de Pasco – smoke and polluted rivers.

You need extra oxygen by now – you're so high up! Snowy peaks tower above you . . . but you find a pass through to the east side of the Andes – and you meet thick tropical forest. Ahead of you lies the mighty Amazon rain forest.

*Can you name the highest mountain in the Andes? (Answer on page 96.)

▶ *The condor is one of the world's largest vultures: its wingspan is up to ten feet. It uses currents of warm air to soar gracefully – then swoops on its prey, often a dead animal. The Andes of Peru, in the background, have very steep slopes.*

▼ *The Incas made superb terraces in their mountain homeland, long before the Spanish conquerors destroyed their empire. The terraces helped farmers and stopped soil erosion. Now Machu Picchu, their "lost city," is one of Peru's main attractions.*

BELIEVE IT OR NOT. . . the world's largest flower is on the world's slowest flowering plant! In Bolivia a rare plant flowers only once in 80 to 150 years – and then dies! But it's worth waiting to see the *Puya raimondii* (if you have a lot of time to spare!) because it's the biggest flower in the world: it's over 6 feet wide and the stem is 30 feet tall – higher than your house! This sounds like an April fool joke – but it's true! If you can't get anyone to believe it, tell them to check it in the *Guinness Book of Records*. One specimen of the flower planted at sea level in a botanical garden in California, USA, in 1958 eventually flowered in 1986 – after just 28 years. . . .

COLORFUL COATS OF ARMS
The national emblems of all the Andes countries feature flags draped around a shield. Like Ecuador and Bolivia, Colombia has a condor perched on top of its very striking coat of arms.

◀ **Ecuador's** official badge shows the snow-covered Andes high above the coast.

▶ **Bolivia** has no coast. The badge shows the Andes mountains above good farmland.

THE GALAPAGOS ISLANDS are a remote group of volcanic islands 620 miles west of Ecuador in the Pacific Ocean (see map page 85). They are very important for wildlife. It was here that Charles Darwin developed his theory of evolution. This Galapagos tortoise is a species found only on these islands. It's important now to conserve the various rare species here and to control the "invaders" – not just rats and cats, but grasses and citrus plants too. WWF is helping with both these projects.

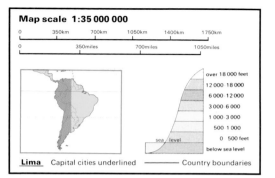

Map scale 1:35 000 000

0	350km	700km	1050km	1400km	1750km
0	350miles		700miles		1050miles

over 18 000 feet
12 000 - 18 000
6 000 - 12 000
3 000 - 6 000
1 000 - 3 000
500 - 1 000
0 - 500 feet
sea level
below sea level

Lima Capital cities underlined ——— Country boundaries

▼ **Llamas,** *like these in Bolivia, don't mind the snow in the high Andes. Some of them have even got snow on their backs, but they have thick, warm wool. Llamas are domesticated animals: you can see a man strapping a bag on to one of them. Bolivia is the poorest country in South America. It has no money for conservation, and the pollution from the tin mines adds poison to beautiful rivers.*

▶ *"Overfishing" off Peru reduced stocks – possibly forever. The fishermen are now poor and unemployed. And the seabirds who used to live on fish are dying. It's a major ecological disaster – yet few people even know about it.*

FISHING OFF PERU: A sad story

The cool ocean current was ideal for fish. Small fishing boats like the ones on the stamp and the photograph caused few problems. But below the four small pictures of fish, there are some worrying phrases in the Spanish language. *"Industria pesquera: Especies industriales"* means "Fishing industry: industrial species."

Bigger boats were used, with bigger nets – and more and more fish were caught. It soon became an "industry." The nets had smaller holes, so even the little fish were caught. Most were not eaten – they were used as fertilizer for farmers' crops in rich countries. What a waste!

Brazil

The Amazon "basin," the world's biggest river system, is the location of the world's biggest tropical forest. The forest isn't only in Brazil: it reaches into Colombia, Peru and Bolivia as well. But it is in Brazil that vast areas are being cut down. The air photograph on page 74 helps to show what is happening.

It isn't all gloom. There are some forest reserves, and the Brazilian government is getting help from WWF and other organizations to develop conservation projects.

Trees are vital. They soak up harmful carbon dioxide from the atmosphere as they grow and release it when they die – very slowly if they decay, instantly if they are burned. Tropical rain forests help control the climate right around the world. Without the Amazon's trees, global warming is much more likely (see page 20).

▲ **The Amazon forest** – the most important rain forest in the world – is being destroyed for timber, mining, cattle ranches, and for small farms. The biggest trees are taken out on new roads and sold; the other trees are burned. What a waste!

▶ **This new forest road** is just a muddy track, but it allows big logs to be taken away and sold. Thousands of tall forest trees have been cut down to make space for this road – and millions more will go along it. You can see an embankment (foreground) and a cutting (background), just like on a motorway.

"SLASH-AND-BURN" AGRICULTURE

I. Clearing the land. . .
This hard work is the first step for hungry families. They need to grow enough food for themselves so they "slash" down and burn the forest vegetation.

2. Planting. . .
Root crops and also banana palms are planted several times a year on the family's plot of land. The work is all done by hand, because any sort of modern machinery is too expensive for the poor people to buy.

3. Harvesting. . .
The first two harvests are usually quite good. But after three or four years the soil becomes exhausted and harvests are poor.

4. Returning the land to forest.
People move on to another new plot, and the old land gradually returns to forest after many years. But the "secondary forest" is not as rich and varied as the original forest. This type of farming certainly damages the environment – but it is not as bad as the damage done by big logging and mining companies, and in the past the forest has survived.

- Over half of all the species of plants in the world are found in rain forests.
- There are more species of plants and insects in four square miles of Amazonia than in all of Britain.
- New species are still being found.
- Many modern medicines come from rain forest plants.
- Over half the world's rain forests have gone in the last 50 years.
- An area the size of Belgium is still being destroyed every year.
- Lots of species are becoming extinct.
- Prospectors looking for gold are poisoning the rivers with mercury.
- The majority of local people don't benefit from the destruction. The land cleared for ranching loses its goodness after a few years because it no longer gets humus from the forest.

◀ **This coatimundi** (a relative of the raccoon) looks happy enough. But he will suffer if more forest is cut down. In fact, his species may not even survive. It isn't just the animals that suffer – flowers, insects and birds are affected too. The people who live there are harmed as well. Some Indian tribes have lived in harmony with the forest for thousands of years; now their way of life is at risk or has already vanished completely.

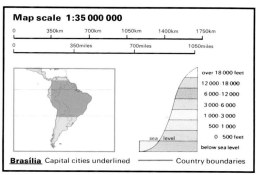

Map scale 1:35 000 000

| over 18 000 feet |
| 12 000 - 18 000 |
| 6 000 - 12 000 |
| 3 000 - 6 000 |
| 1 000 - 3 000 |
| 500 - 1 000 |
| 0 - 500 feet |
| below sea level |

Brasília Capital cities underlined ⎯⎯ Country boundaries

▶ **This Brazilian family** – and their donkey – lives in the northeast of the huge country. This is a dry area, with thorn bushes and tall grass, rather like the savanna of Africa. Many people live here, but it is hard to make a living. Some people have moved to the big cities on the coast, and others have moved to the Amazon forest as settlers and prospectors.

INGREDIENTS:
PACIFIC PILCHARDS
TOMATO SAUCE

Packed for:
GLENRYCK (U.K.) LTD.,
P.O. BOX 22,
8 FRIDAY STREET,
HENLEY-ON-THAMES,
RG9 1 AH

PRODUCT OF CHILE

◀ *The world of food.* *The next time you go to a supermarket, why not look at where the food comes from? We discovered these "Pacific pilchards" from Chile, and there were "Pacific pilchards" from Thailand, too – half a world away, but still the same ocean! Tuna fish come from even more countries. Try to find tins labeled "dolphin friendly": they will contain fish that have been caught in ways that do not trap and kill these intelligent creatures.*

▶ *The port of San Antonio, Chile.*
Seabirds are always glad when the fishing boats come home: perhaps the fishermen will throw unwanted fish over the side of the boat. The cold Humboldt current off the South American coast has for centuries provided a livelihood for millions of families in Chile and Peru. San Antonio is on the Pacific coast near Santiago, the Chilean capital.

To understand this part of the world, it's vital to know whether it rains or not. Rain clouds hardly ever cross the Andes – they drop all their rain there. One side of the Andes is wet; the other side is dry.

But which is the "dry side"? It's not an easy answer – because the answer is different in different places! Northern Chile is very dry indeed – because the wet winds come from the east. Central Chile has rain in winter, but has hot, dry summers – much like southern Europe. Southern Chile is very wet all year – because the wet winds come from the west. There are thick forests in most of southern Chile.

Argentina is the opposite of Chile. Most of northern Argentina has plenty of rain, and the grasslands called the "pampas" make good farmland. But Patagonia, in southern Argentina, is a cool desert, with thorn bushes for vegetation. This is a windswept area, with more sheep than people. Wildlife has to be hardy to survive here; a burrow comes in very useful.

▼ *Patagonia,* in southern Argentina, is a harsh and dry landscape, but it has a beauty all of its own. Very few people live here, and even fewer people visit this cold, windy area. There are thorn bushes in the foreground, but the mountains in the background are almost bare. A hard layer of rock has made the tops of the mountains almost as flat as a table. In fact, the Argentinians call the area the Central Meseta – "meseta" is Spanish for "little table." Patagonia is a "cool desert."

◀ **The dense forests of southern Chile** have many rare and beautiful trees. It's one of the least visited parts of the world – but you can often find a "Chilean pine" in suburban gardens. It's now called the "monkey puzzle" tree... because it would puzzle a monkey. Even in Chile, however, the forests are now being cut down for woodpulp for export to Japan. There's nowhere else like Chile and Argentina. The map below stretches to 55° south of the Equator. By comparison, Africa's most southern point is at a warm 35° south, and the Australian mainland ends at 39° south; so South America reaches much further south toward the Antarctic than the other continents. In fact, it's the only continent that reaches the really cool latitudes in the Southern Hemisphere (except for Antarctica itself, of course!).

▼ **A hairy armadillo** in Argentina. "Armadillo" means "small armor," and he really is armor-plated, with skin that is as hard as the horns of other animals. He moves slowly, so the "armor" helps him survive when he meets hostile animals.

Map scale 1:35 000 000

| 0 | 350km | 700km | 1050km |

| 0 | 350miles | 700miles |

Country boundaries
Santiago Capital cities underlined

over 18 000 feet
12 000 - 18 000
6 000 - 12 000
3 000 - 6 000
1 000 - 3 000
500 - 1 000
0 - 500 feet
sea level
below sea level

WHAT DO THE SPANISH NAMES MEAN?
Argentina: "Land of silver mines" (until all the silver ran out)
Buenos Aires: "Good air" (until the gasoline fumes arrived)
Montevideo: "I see a mountain" (even though there isn't one!)
Tierra del Fuego: "Land of fire" (plenty of volcanoes?)

THE FALKLANDS
The Falkland Islands (called *Islas Malvinas* by the Argentinians) are cold and windy. Very few people live in this harsh environment – but there are lots of sheep and the wildlife is superb. This stamp (right) was issued

to help the rebuilding after the 1982 war between Britain and Argentina over the islands, who both claim ownership. The islands are a wonderful place to see penguins, seals and albatrosses – the bird with the world's biggest wingspan. The wild birds seem almost tame because they have so few enemies.

The South Atlantic Ocean is rich in fish, and the stamp (left) shows a gray-tailed skate. Some of the fish in the seas around the Falkland Islands provide food for the seabirds. But, even in this remote area, trawlers from faraway Japan have been accused of overfishing. Nowhere seems safe now from the greed of people and businesses.

Australia

Australia has been an island for about 50 million years, and many species of plants and animals are found only there. Most Australian animals are "marsupials": that means they have a pouch for their baby. Several species of marsupial are now endangered – such as the greater bilby and the hairy-nosed wombat.

There are only about 18 million people on this huge island – and most of them live in cities, so there are fewer environmental problems than in many other countries.

The north of Australia is tropical, the center is desert or bush, and much of the south is temperate, so there is a great variety of environments. The island of Tasmania, the country's sixth state, also has its own special plants and insects.

▲ **Koalas** live in eucalyptus (gum) trees. These trees give them all the food they need, and they spend most of the day and night there. Koalas are marsupials, so they are NOT bears – even though almost everyone calls them bears! There were once millions of koalas, but they were killed mercilessly: in the 1920s, two million koala skins were exported every year. Now, thankfully, they are a protected species.

▶ **The red kangaroo** is the biggest marsupial in the world. Can you spot her "joey" in her pouch? It lives there for about six months – it must be one of the safest environments in the world! The baby is less than an inch long when it's born. The adult can weigh 70 kg, as much as an adult human, and bound along at 25 miles per hour. The 55 species of kangaroo and wallaby live mainly on the plains of Australia. The numbers are now growing, but some species are still endangered.

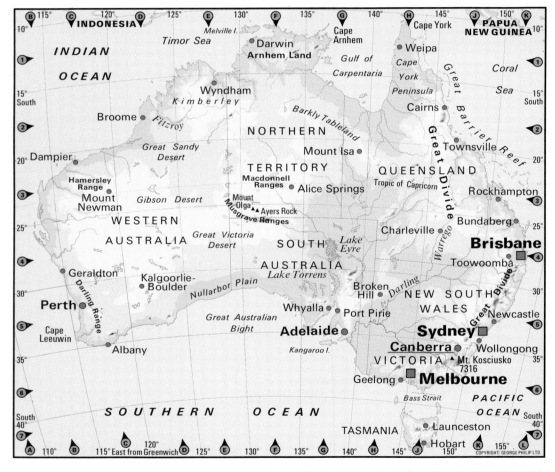

MARSUPIALS ON MONEY
1-cent coin: a "sugar glider"
5-cent coin: a spiny anteater echidna

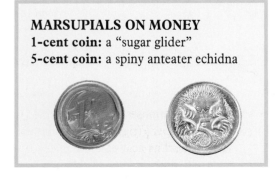

Map scale 1:30 000 000

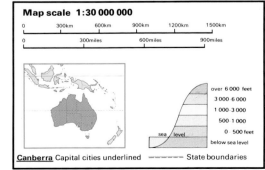

Canberra Capital cities underlined ----- State boundaries

▶ **The Olga Mountains** in the center of Australia, seen from the air. They are the last remnants of a great mountain range. The mountains are red. The land is far from dead, even though it is often called "the dead heart" of Australia. Many special plants can survive in this hot dry climate, and the Aborigines could find enough food to live here. This area, west of the famous Ayers Rock, is now a national park, and it has special protection.

▼ **The Great Barrier Reef** is also very much alive! This 1,200-mile-long "Marine Park," made of coral, is the world's biggest protected marine (sea) area. There are over 400 types of coral here. When coral is alive, it sways gently in the sea currents; when it dies, it forms hard coral "limestone" rock. The 1,500 species of fish include the yellow ones shown here (called "damsels") and the blue-green ones ("pullers").

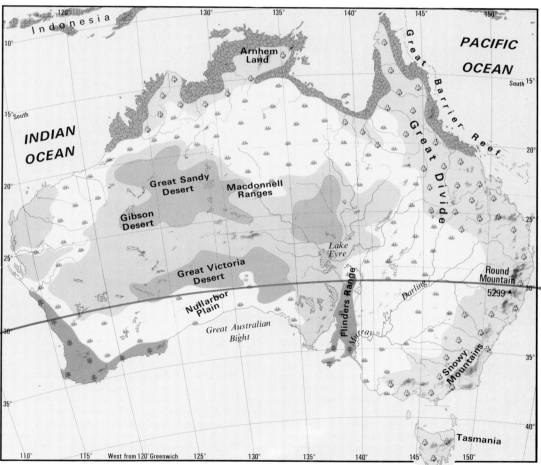

	Tropical rain forest
	Deciduous forest
	'Mediterranean' vegetation
	Grassland and scrub
	Semi-desert
	Desert

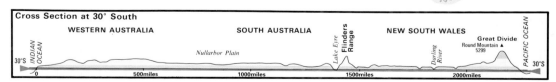

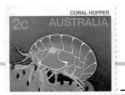

REEF LIFE. Octopuses (far left) visit the Great Barrier Reef, home to the "coral hopper" (right). But the "crown of thorns" starfish (left) has invaded – and its acid digestive juices are destroying the coral.

The Pacific

Many people feel that parts of the Pacific Ocean are the nearest we get to "paradise on Earth": one country even has a bird-of-paradise on its flag (see next page). The sea is warm, the sun is hot, and coconut palms give shade on the beautiful beaches.

But there are some problems, especially those caused by its mineral deposits. For example, mining of copper on Bougainville (square J8), mining of nickel and chrome on New Caledonia (square K10), and mining of phosphates on Ocean Island and Nauru (square K8) have all polluted the land and the water.

Testing of nuclear weapons by the USA and France over many years has caused dangerous pollution, and the full effects may not yet be known. Imported plants and animals may threaten the special plants and animals of various Pacific islands.

◀ **Coral islands** ▲ There are many thousands of lovely coral islands in the Pacific Ocean. From a ship (above) all you see is a thin white stripe (the beach), trees and some buildings... but from the air (left), it all makes sense: you can see the coral just below the sea, and the round shape of an atoll. Both these islands belong to Fiji (square L9). If sea levels rise and storms get stronger, many of these atolls could be covered by the sea if the Greenhouse Effect continues to happen (see page 20). Nauru (square K8) could be the first country in the world to "disappear."

▲ **Volcanic islands.** Some islands in the Pacific Ocean were made by volcanoes. They are mountainous, and most of them have dense forest on the fertile soil. This photograph shows Papeete, on Tahiti (square Q9) – an island being discovered by rich tourists and by around-the-world travelers. People who live on "high" islands have less to fear from the Greenhouse Effect and global warming. Many of the volcanic islands are fringed by coral reefs. Most of the world's active volcanoes are around the edge of the Pacific Ocean.

[For key see Australia map on page 82.]

◀ **NEW ZEALAND** has many special plants and animals. The flightless kiwi (20-cent coin) only comes out at night. The kakapo (30-cent stamp) was threatened with extinction by rats brought from Europe. The birds have been saved by being moved to a small island with no rats. The stamp also shows native New Zealand ferns.

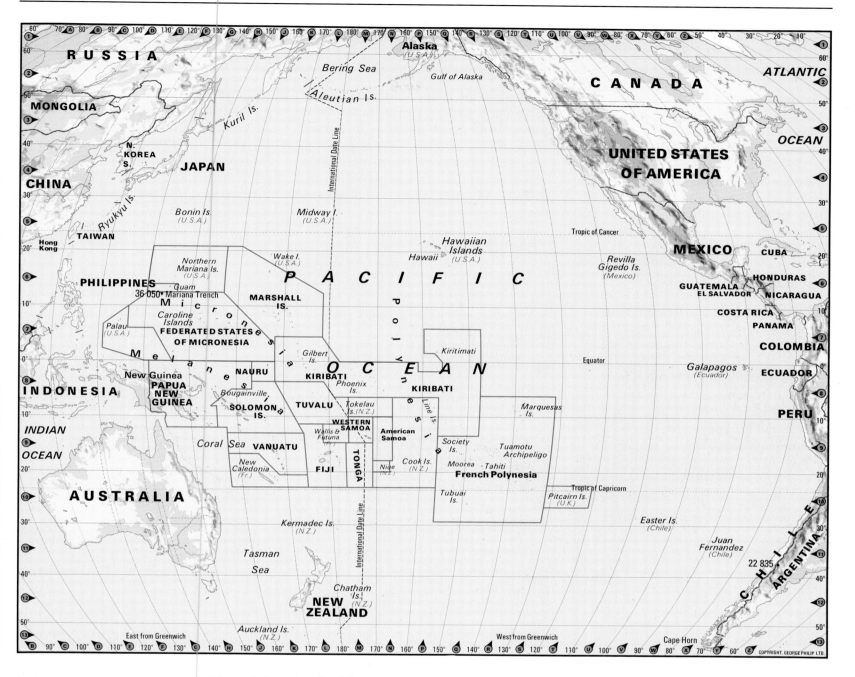

The mighty Pacific map showing the Pacific Ocean region with the following labels:

RUSSIA, MONGOLIA, CHINA, N. KOREA, S. KOREA, JAPAN, TAIWAN, Hong Kong, PHILIPPINES, INDONESIA, AUSTRALIA, NEW ZEALAND

Alaska (U.S.A.), Bering Sea, Gulf of Alaska, Aleutian Is., Kuril Is., CANADA, ATLANTIC OCEAN, UNITED STATES OF AMERICA, Tropic of Cancer, MEXICO, CUBA, GUATEMALA, EL SALVADOR, HONDURAS, NICARAGUA, COSTA RICA, PANAMA, COLOMBIA, ECUADOR, PERU, CHILE, ARGENTINA

Ryukyu Is., Bonin Is. (U.S.A.), Midway I. (U.S.A.), Hawaiian Islands (U.S.A.), Hawaii, Revilla Gigedo Is. (Mexico), Wake I. (U.S.A.), Northern Mariana Is. (U.S.A.), Guam, 36 050 Mariana Trench, Micronesia, MARSHALL IS., PACIFIC OCEAN, Caroline Islands, Palau (U.S.A.), FEDERATED STATES OF MICRONESIA, Melanesia, Gilbert Is., Kiritimati, Equator, Galapagos (Ecuador)

New Guinea, PAPUA NEW GUINEA, NAURU, KIRIBATI, Phoenix Is., KIRIBATI, Bougainville, SOLOMON IS., TUVALU, Tokelau Is.(N.Z.), Marquesas Is., Line Is., WESTERN SAMOA, Wallis & Futuna, American Samoa, Society Is., Tuamotu Archipeligo, INDIAN OCEAN, Coral Sea, VANUATU, New Caledonia (Fr.), FIJI, TONGA, Niue (N.Z.), Cook Is. (N.Z.), Moorea, Tahiti, French Polynesia, Polynesia

Tropic of Capricorn, Tubuai Is., Pitcairn Is. (U.K.), Easter Is. (Chile), Juan Fernandez (Chile), 22 835

Tasman Sea, Kermadec Is. (N.Z.), International Date Line, Chatham Is. (N.Z.)

East from Greenwich, West from Greenwich, Auckland Is. (N.Z.), Cape Horn

COPYRIGHT. GEORGE PHILIP LTD.

▲ **The mighty Pacific.** This map covers a much greater area than any other in this atlas – apart from the world maps on pages 2 to 23. The Pacific is bigger than the Atlantic Ocean and the Indian Ocean combined (see page 8).
- "MICRONESIA" means "tiny islands."
- "MELANESIA" means "islands of black-skinned people."
- "POLYNESIA" means "many islands."

▲ **The flag of Papua New Guinea** shows a bird-of-paradise and the "Southern Cross": stars that are seen in the Southern Hemisphere. These stars are also on the flags of Australia and New Zealand. "PNG" is an independent country, but only half the island of New Guinea.

▶ **Fiji's coat of arms** shows four important foods that grow in its fertile soils. Can you spot them? Here are two clues: ignore the dove, but look at what the lion is holding! (Answer on page 96.)

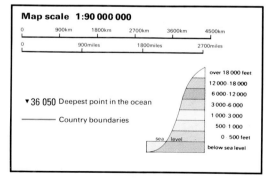

Map scale 1:90 000 000

| 0 | 900km | 1800km | 2700km | 3600km | 4500km |

| 0 | 900miles | 1800miles | 2700miles |

over 18 000 feet
12 000-18 000
6 000-12 000
3 000-6 000
1 000-3 000
500-1 000
0-500 feet
sea level
below sea level

▼ 36 050 Deepest point in the ocean

—— Country boundaries

DID YOU KNOW? The world's largest butterfly, Queen Alexandra's birdwing, is found in New Guinea. The largest moth lives there, too – the "Hercules." Both can have a wingspan of up to 11 inches.

The Arctic

The Arctic lands have a tundra landscape that is easily damaged. In summer, the tundra is marshy because the subsoil is still frozen. This is called "permafrost" – short for "PERMAnent FROST." The small plants of the tundra – mosses, lichens, grasses and small shrubs – can be destroyed by footsteps. Yet in winter, nature is more powerful than people: the severe frosts destroy road surfaces and buckle railroad tracks. So all developments in the Arctic – for mining, airfields, fishing or tourism – must fit in with the special features of the tundra habitat. Otherwise people damage nature in the summer, and nature damages new developments in the winter.

WHICH DIRECTION IS SOUTH?
This map and the Antarctica map (page 89) are the only ones in the atlas which don't have north at the top. At the North Pole, every direction is south! Your compass is useless.

THE "NORTHWEST PASSAGE"
This is the route around the north of Canada from the Atlantic to the Bering Strait, which separates Asia and North America. Explorers hoped it would be a route to the Pacific – but it's too icy.

COUNTRIES OF THE ARCTIC
North America: Canada, USA (state of Alaska), Greenland
Asia and Europe: Russia
Europe: Norway, Iceland
Now the "cold war" is over, these six countries are working together to study and conserve the Arctic environment.

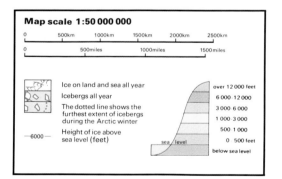

Map scale 1:50 000 000

0	500km	1000km	1500km	2000km	2500km
0		500miles		1000miles	1500miles

Ice on land and sea all year
Icebergs all year
The dotted line shows the furthest extent of icebergs during the Arctic winter
Height of ice above sea level (feet)

over 12 000 feet
6 000 - 12 000
3 000 - 6 000
1 000 - 3 000
500 - 1 000
0 - 500 feet
sea / level
below sea level

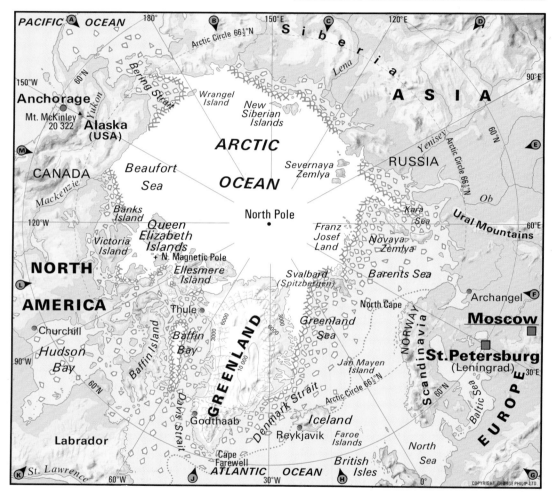

THE "WINDCHILL FACTOR"
The stronger the wind, the colder the same temperature feels. The chart shows the effect of the wind: for example, a temperature of 14° Fahrenheit *feels* like −27°F if there's a wind blowing at about 25 miles per hour (mph). The danger of frostbite is therefore much greater, so explorers and scientists need to know this before they travel in the Arctic. It applies, on a less severe scale, to you in winter!

Local temperature (°F)	32°	23	14	5	−4	−13	−22	−31	−40	−49	−58
Wind speed (mph)	**Windchill equivalent temperature °F**										
10	18	7	−4	−15	−26	−36	−47	−60	−71	−87	−92
20	7	−6	−18	−33	−44	−56	−71	−83	−96	−108	−121
30	1	−13	−27	−40	−54	−69	−81	−98	−108	−123	−137
40	−2	−17	−31	−45	−60	−74	−87	−101	−116	−130	−144
50	−4	−18	−33	−47	−62	−76	−90	−105	−119	−134	−148

Little danger for properly clothed persons   *Considerable . . .*   *Very great . . .*
. . . danger of exposed skin freezing

*◄ **Scientists test the water quality** of the Arctic Ocean. Pollution is a problem, even in the Arctic. Ships can only travel on the Arctic Ocean in the long days of summer, when some of the ice melts. The Arctic Ocean is the world's smallest ocean – but even so it's huge: 50 times bigger than the UK, five times bigger than India, and twice as big as Australia.*

DID YOU KNOW that Greenland was given its name to persuade Vikings to go and live in that icy land over 1,000 years ago? So there's nothing new about telling lies about a place to encourage visitors!

*▼ **Greenland in summer.** Small parts of Greenland ARE green in the short summer season. But most of Greenland is a massive ice cap: you can see part of it in the background. On page 10, there's a graph of Greenland's amazing climate (Eismitte). Only about 59,000 people live in Greenland. It now governs itself – but Denmark still controls defense and foreign policy.*

THE WORLD'S BIGGEST FLOODS

Three of the world's ten longest rivers flow northward through Russia to the Arctic Ocean: the Yenisey (3,450 miles), the Ob (3,200 miles) and the Lena (3,000 miles). The length of each river is *twice* as far as from London to the Sahara Desert!

Spring comes to the south sooner than to the north. The mouths of these rivers are the last parts to melt. The rest of the rivers, swollen with "meltwater," flow toward the still-frozen Arctic Ocean. The result is the world's biggest floods – every spring. The resulting wetlands are ideal for migrating birds.

*◄ **These polar bears** prefer the ice floes to the mountainous land in the background on Svalbard, an Arctic island that belongs to Norway. But in some places, polar bears have discovered the joys of tipping out dustbins to find tasty food: it's much easier than fishing! This is now a big problem in the town of Churchill, beside Hudson Bay in Canada. Some bears are even put in "jail" for the night, and then taken far away by truck before being released. Some people feel that this is wrong: it's the fault of humans, not polar bears, that there's waste food to collect. But this is another example of a wild creature adapting to its changing environment in order to survive – like the smart "urban" fox pictured on page 28.*

The Antarctic

Antarctica is twice as big in June (winter) as it is in December (summer)! In summer, much of the sea ice melts. It has *no* land animals – but is "home" to vast numbers of birds and mammals. About 800 people live there in winter, and up to 3,000 people in the summer. But there are *no* people living there permanently, and *no* children!

The American McMurdo Base is the biggest "town." It has a huge rubbish dump, with chemicals leaking from barrels. Untreated sewage pollutes the harbor.

There are huge amounts of valuable minerals in Antarctica – coal, oil, gold, silver, copper and lead. But if they were mined, much more pollution would come. In 1991 all the countries involved agreed to a 50-year ban on any mining there... *great news!*

▶ *Lonely beauty at Barne Glacier. The silence is broken by great crashes when ice falls from high on the ice cliff.*

▲ *Rothera Island. Dog sledges were used in Antarctica for many years, but the Antarctic Treaty now bans "alien species" except for man. The last huskies left in 1994. You can see that the continent is not all ice: 2% (one-fiftieth) of Antarctica is free of ice in the 24-hour daylight of summer.*

WHO OWNS "THE LAST WILDERNESS"?

There were lots of claims to Antarctica – each one was shaped like a slice of cake. These stamps show the Australian claims (left) and  Chile's claim (right). But in 1961 all the claims were "frozen": an ideal way to preserve a frozen continent! The Antarctic Treaty states that Antarctica should be used only for peaceful cooperation and scientific research, and not exploited for making money.

TRANSPORT IN ANTARCTICA

Dog sledges (left) have been replaced by the skidoo (right, like a motorbike on skis), caterpillar tractors (like the French one below – heavy to dig out of drifts!) and speedy helicopters and airplanes (below).

PUZZLE STAMP...

How did this New Zealand geologist get to this part of Antarctica? What has he found? And why is it an important scientific discovery? (Answers on page 96.)

◀ **Penguins cannot fly** – even though they are birds. But they are strong swimmers and can swim as fast as 25 miles an hour. These are King penguins.

▼ **If the polar ice melts** due to global warming (see page 21), most of Antarctica would disappear. The cross section shows that most of the land there is below sea level. Only a few mountain ridges would remain as islands. Sea levels worldwide would rise, and every seaside town would be partly or wholly under water. Some island countries would vanish. . . .

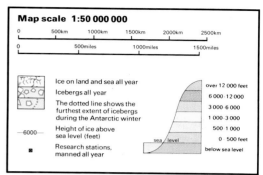

Map scale 1:50 000 000

| 0 | 500km | 1000km | 1500km | 2000km | 2500km |
| 0 | 500miles | 1000miles | 1500miles |

Ice on land and sea all year
Icebergs all year
The dotted line shows the furthest extent of icebergs during the Antarctic winter
—6000— Height of ice above sea level (feet)
■ Research stations, manned all year

over 12 000 feet
6 000-12 000
3 000-6 000
1 000-3 000
500-1 000
0-500 feet
below sea level
sea level

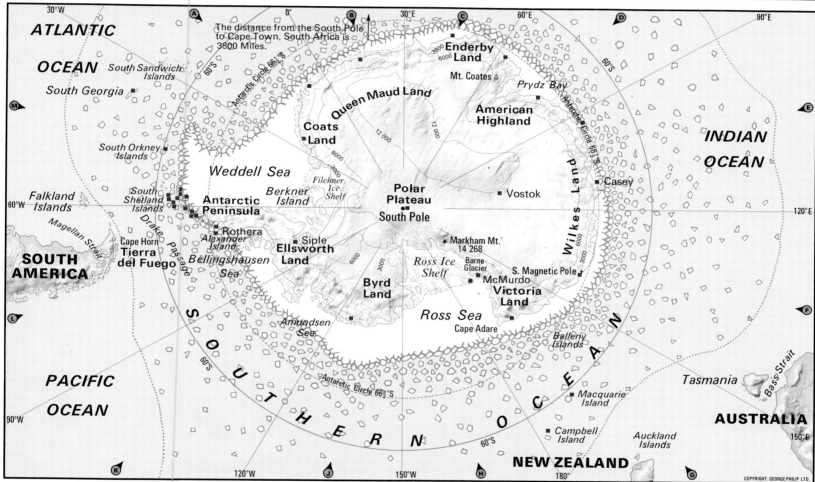

ATLANTIC OCEAN

The distance from the South Pole to Cape Town, South Africa is 3800 Miles.

South Sandwich Islands
South Georgia
South Orkney Islands
Weddell Sea
Falkland Islands
Magellan Strait
South Shetland Islands
Cape Horn
Tierra del Fuego
Drake Passage
Alexander Island
Rothera
Bellingshausen Sea
Antarctic Peninsula
Berkner Island
Filchner Ice Shelf
Coats Land
Queen Maud Land
Enderby Land
Mt. Coates
Prydz Bay
American Highland
Casey
Polar Plateau
South Pole
Vostok
Siple
Ellsworth Land
Byrd Land
Markham Mt. 14 268
Ross Ice Shelf
Barne Glacier
S. Magnetic Sole
McMurdo
Victoria Land
Wilkes Land
INDIAN OCEAN
SOUTH AMERICA
PACIFIC OCEAN
Amundsen Sea
Ross Sea
Cape Adare
Balleny Islands
SOUTHERN OCEAN
Macquarie Island
Tasmania
Bass Strait
AUSTRALIA
Campbell Island
Auckland Islands
NEW ZEALAND
Antarctic Circle 66½°S
COPYRIGHT GEORGE PHILIP LTD.

CROSS SECTION OF ANTARCTICA (from Siple to Casey)

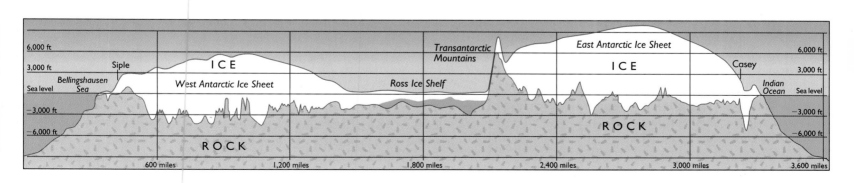

6,000 ft
3,000 ft
Sea level
–3,000 ft
–6,000 ft

Siple
Bellingshausen Sea
West Antarctic Ice Sheet
ICE
Ross Ice Shelf
Transantarctic Mountains
East Antarctic Ice Sheet
ICE
Casey
Indian Ocean
ROCK

600 miles 1,200 miles 1,800 miles 2,400 miles 3,000 miles 3,600 miles

The world's future

Will the news in the future be bad – more pollution . . . more wars . . . more species becoming extinct – or can there be some good news too?

We don't know what the future holds – but we can all try to make a better world. These pages focus mainly on the good news and good ideas. Often, it's not a simple case of "good or bad": a good idea can have some bad side effects, as the photographs on this page show.

There are always some questions you can ask at school. For example:
● Do we recycle all the waste paper? Could it be put in special bins and collected?
● Could your school plant a bush from every continent? It could become your "World Garden." It would help the birds, as well as making the world more real for all the children to understand.
● Does your school have good books and other information on the environment?

▲ **The power of the wind** is pure, clean and free. People have used sails, windmills and windpumps for years – now the wind can be used for making electricity with no pollution. BUT it's an ugly landscape, it wastes lots of precious space, and it makes only a small amount of electricity.

▼ **The power of the sun** is pure, clean and free, too. "Solar power" has been used for making raisins (sun-dried grapes) and salt (evaporated seawater) for thousands of years. Now it can be used for electricity, by using reflectors. BUT it's only a solution for richer people in warm countries.

THE UNITED NATIONS
The olive branches around the globe on the UN flag are symbols of world peace. Can you recognize six continents on the map – and see which one is missing?★ And can you name the official UN languages on the stamp?★ The UN agencies do lots of good work to make a better world. How many of these can you name?★ UNEP, UNESCO, FAO, WHO. The UN is involved in the vital areas of environment, education, science, culture, food, agriculture, and world health, among others.
(★ Answers on page 96.)

MAKE UP YOUR OWN SLOGAN! A slogan can be worth a thousand words, if it's a good one. Below is an important environmental slogan★, and on the right is a rhyming one from Trinidad in the West Indies. Now we need a slogan to tell us that all animals and plants are precious. One for our world is "HANDLE WITH CARE!" ★It's in German: look at the picture behind to help you guess what it says.
(Answer on page 96.)

► **Oceans in danger.** *Spills from oil tankers (like the Exxon Valdez off Alaska), dirty rivers and industrial waste are all polluting the oceans. Will action be taken to control the mess worldwide?*

▼ **Animals in danger.** *Everyone knows about "endangered species." But it's not only the well-known animals, such as these black rhinoceroses in Tanzania, that are at risk. More than 4,500 species are on the danger list, and more are added to it every year.*

DID YOU KNOW? The most common bird that has ever lived became extinct in 1914 – the North American passenger pigeon. Millions were killed, for food and for sport. Now they are gone forever – and you cannot ever bring a species back to life.

WHAT CAN WE DO TO HELP?
More than you think! Here are some ideas for saving energy:
- Try to cycle more: only "human energy" is used!
- Ask adults to use cars less: public transport is far less wasteful.
- Advise your parents to install lots of insulation and draft proofing in your house: it's easy, cheap – and cosy too.
- Turn the heating down (it's probably too high).
- Switch off the lights if not needed, and use low-energy light bulbs.
- Become a vegetarian for a week. You might enjoy it!

And here are some other ideas for things to check at home:
- Is the bleach for the drains "biodegradable"?
- Are the spray cans used in the house and garden "ozone friendly"?
- Do we have to use poisons to kill pests such as the greenfly? These can harm other garden creatures, including birds.

▼ **Check the label.** *If you eat tuna fish, look for a "dolphin friendly" label – like this one from Thailand in Southeast Asia.*

HABITATS IN DANGER
It's not only animals that are at risk: complete habitats are at risk as well. If the habitat is destroyed, many species could be threatened: not just animals, but plants too. For example, the great variety of butterflies will suffer if their favorite plants become rare. The Kenyan butterfly on this stamp is shown with the plant it likes. If the plant dies out, so could the butterfly.

Kenya 4/

Papilio phorcas
PAKU KIJANI

The people of the world could conserve plants and animals – it's a question of deciding what our priorities are. You can help, even if the habitat is thousands of miles away:
- If you buy cacti or bulbs ask the people in the shop or garden center if they were "stolen" from a wild habitat.
- Ask grown-ups not to buy items made from tropical hardwood, unless the wood is from a well-managed area.
- Join an international environmental organization.

Sainsbury's South Seas Tuna is specially selected from Pacific catches. Its light fresh colour and delicate taste makes it ideal for salads, pâtés, pizzas, dips or vol-au-vent filling. 190

SAINSBURY'S TUNA IS CAUGHT WITH A POLE AND LINE (RATHER THAN BEING TRAWLED) THUS AVOIDING DANGER TO OTHER MARINE LIFE

SAINSBURY'S
South Seas TUNA STEAK
lightmeat tuna in brine
HIGH PROTEIN

► **Don't buy souvenirs** *such as tropical shells unless you're certain that you're not destroying a species. The conch shell on this stamp comes from Vanuatu, in the South Pacific (see map page 85). Few people have yet realized the link between souvenir buying and the destruction of habitats – so here's another suggestion: tell other people about your good ideas!*

IF WE ALL WORK TOGETHER...
...WE CAN HELP TO SAVE THE WORLD AFTER ALL!

INDEX

The first number given after each name is the page number; then a letter and another number tell you which square of the map you should look at. For example, Aachen is in square A3 on page 32. Find A at the top or bottom of the map on page 32 and put a finger on it. Put another finger on the number 3 at the side of the map. Move your fingers in from the edge of the map and they will meet in square A3. Aachen will now be easy to find. It is a city on the western borders of Germany.

If a name goes through more than one square, the square given in the index is the one in which the biggest part of the name falls.

Names like *Gulf of Mexico* and *Cape Horn* are in the index as *Mexico, Gulf of* and *Horn, Cape*.

A D-I-Y QUIZ: Choose a group of ten names in the index. Challenge a friend: which of you knows where more places are on the maps?

Answers to questions

11. Puzzle picture
The photograph shows giant hailstones in Johannesburg, South Africa's largest city. They fell on a roof and are shooting out of a drain-pipe, making a big heap. A gold-colored coin has been put in the picture to give a scale. This hailstorm came at the end of the dry season.

12. How a seismograph works
A weight (center) is attached to a delicate spring (top). When an earthquake comes, the spring moves, and the pen (at left) "scribbles" on paper on a rotating drum (blue on the diagram): the bigger the shock, the bigger the scribble.

12. Puzzle stamps
Top: North America (left), Europe (center), Asia (right).
Bottom: South America (left), Africa, Antarctica, Australia (right).
The ostrich lives in Africa, the emu in Australia.

24. Puzzle stamp from Helvetia
• Languages: German, French and Italian.
• Slogan: "Protection of the natural environment: SURVIVE!"
• Country: Switzerland ("Helvetia" was the Latin name for the country).
• Picture messages: Clean air – for birds; Pure earth – for people and trees; Clear water (rain and rivers) for healthy fish.
• The "odd one out" is fire: it shows the "bad news" of destruction and pollution.

25. European animals and birds
Reindeer, otter; European bison, fallow deer; wild boar, peregrine falcon; pheasant; badger; alpine ibex; pelican; octopus (Mediterranean Sea).

26. The Baltic Sea
The three Scandinavian countries that have a Baltic coastline are Denmark, Sweden and Finland. The other six countries that share the Baltic Sea are Germany, Poland, Russia, Lithuania, Latvia and Estonia.

32. Slogan on German stamp
SCHÜTZT DIE NATUR means "Protect nature" or "Protect the environment."

34. The Mediterranean Sea
The European countries that border the Mediterranean are Spain, France, Monaco, Italy, Albania and Greece. If the Adriatic Sea is included, there are also Slovenia, Croatia, Bosnia and Yugoslavia. The African countries are Morocco, Algeria, Tunisia, Libya and Egypt. The Asian countries are Turkey, Syria, Lebanon and Israel.

39. Zoo animals
Top left: Elephants are on page 58, photographed in Tanzania. These are African elephants, but the ones on the stamp are Indian elephants (note the smaller ears!). Bottom left: Seals are on page 24, photographed off the Netherlands. Top right: Przewalski's Horse is on page 49, native to Mongolia. Bottom right: Polar bears are on page 87, photographed in Canada, and on page 42.

40. Asian map question
• West of Asia is Europe.
• Southwest of Asia is Africa.
• To the southeast is Australia.
• Beyond the top is North America.
• Beyond the bottom of the map is Antarctica.

52. Migrating storks
The shadows on the ground are all black; the birds themselves have a white patch.

57. Gorilla sticker
The words are in French because that is the national language of Zaïre. They mean "KAHUZI-BIEGA NATIONAL PARK. Zaïre Institute for Nature Conservation."

65. Canadian provinces
From west to east: British Columbia, Alberta, Saskatchewan, Manitoba, Ontario, Quebec and Newfoundland.

72. Countries of Central America
1 — no coastline on the Pacific: Belize.
2 — no Caribbean coast: El Salvador.
3 — partly outside the tropics: Mexico.
4 — smallest countries: El Salvador, Belize (Belize is very slightly bigger).
5 — famous canal: Panama.

73. Caribbean Islands
1 — the biggest: Cuba.
2 — nearest to the USA: Cuba.
3 — nearest to Honduras: the Cayman Islands. The nearest large island is Jamaica.
4 — nearest to South America: Trinidad.
5 — belongs to the Netherlands: Curaçao (several others are also Dutch).
6 — belongs to France: Guadeloupe and Martinique – both answers are correct.
7 — shared by two countries: Hispaniola, shared by Haiti and the Dominican Republic.

74. Brazil's neighbors
Andean countries: Venezuela, Colombia, Ecuador, Peru, Bolivia, Chile, Argentina.
Ecuador and **Chile** do not border Brazil.

76. Highest mountain in the Andes
The highest peak in the Andes is Aconcagua, in Argentina but very close to the border with Chile. At 22,835 feet it is the highest point on Earth outside central Asia.

85. Fiji's coat of arms
Top: Cocoa pod (held by a lion, which doesn't belong in Fiji). Center left: Sugarcane. Center right: Coconut palm. (Bottom left: Dove of peace). Bottom right: Bananas.

88. Scientists in Antarctica
A geologist is a man who studies rocks. This one has traveled by "skidoo." He has found a rock with the imprint of a fossil plant. This is important because it shows that Antarctica once had a much warmer climate.

90. The United Nations
Americas are on left of flag; Africa at the bottom; Asia and Australisia at the top. So Antarctica is missing. The UN languages on the stamps are English, Russian, Spanish, French and Chinese. The agencies are *UN Environment Program*; *UN Educational, Scientific and Cultural Organization*; *Food and Agriculture Organization*; *World Health Organization*.

90. Slogan on German stamp
"Verhütet Waldbrände" means "Prevent forests burning!"

PHOTOGRAPHIC ACKNOWLEDGMENTS

Andes Press Agency: p. 80 (TR).
Heather Angel/Biofotos: pp. 5 (T &C), 6 (T & B), 17 (L & R), 35 (MR), 52 (BR), 58 (T), 60 (BL), 64 (BR), 70, 74 (T), 82 (T), 83 (L), 87 (M).
Ardea London: pp. 15 (BL), 36 (ML), 80 (BR).
Barnaby's Picture Library: pp. 40 (B), 45 (BL).
Camera Press: pp. 42 (BR), 43 (L).
J. Allan Cash Ltd: pp. 27, 48 (MC), 49 (TL), 55 (BL).
Bruce Coleman Ltd: pp. 16 (L), 19 (MC), 28, 30 (BL), 33 (TL), 35 (ML – both), 36 (MR), 42 (BL), 45 (TR), 62 (MR & BL), 64 (MR & BL), 71 (T), 72 (TR), 79 (ML & BR), 81 (L & R), 84 (MR).
Colorific: p. 12.
Environmental Picture Library: pp. 19 (MR), 32 (B), 46 (T).
Susan Griggs Agency: pp. 23 (B), 46 (B).

Pictor International: p. 49 (MR).
Planet Earth: p. 63.
Rex Features: p. 91 (TR).
RSPB: p. 52 (MR).
Science Photo Library: pp. 35 (BM), 40 (T), 55 (BR).
SCR Library: p. 42 (TR).
Sygma: pp. 38 (T), 43 (BM).
TCL Stock Directory: p. 20.
Tony Stone Worldwide: pp. 13 (B), 14 (T), 15 (MR), 16 (BR), 21 (ML & BL), 23 (TL & TR), 29 (BL), 30 (TL & TR), 32 (R), 36 (B), 42 (BM), 45 (BL), 48 (BR), 54 (TL), 64 (TR), 67 (ML & BR), 69 (M), 71 (B), 72 (BR), 76 (T), 82 (L), 83 (T), 84 (ML), 87 (T), 88 (T & L), 90 (T & C).
Wildlife Matters: pp. 50 (TR), 60 (BR).
WWF International: pp. 8, 11 (BR), 14 (B), 19 (BM), 24 (MR), 26 (MC & MR), 38 (B), 44 (T), 47, 48 (T), 50 (TL), 51 (TL), 52 (T),

54 (ML & BL), 56 (MR & B), 58 (B), 60 (ML), 61 (TR & ML), 74 (B), 76 (BL), 77 (MR), 78 (TL & MR), 87 (B).
WWF UK: pp. 10, 26 (TL), 59, 60 (TR), 72 (ML), 75, 89, 91.
David Wright: pp. 11 (BL & BM), 13 (T), 15 (BR – both), 18, 19 (MR), 21 (BR), 24 (BL & BR), 26 (BL & BR), 29 (TL, TR & ML), 30 (MR), 33 (ML, TR, Mr & BL), 35 (TR), 36 (TM), 38 (L), 44 (B), 51 (ML), 54 (MR & BR), 67 (TR), 68 (BL & BR), 69 (BL & BM), 73 (MC, MR & BR), 84 (TR).
Zefa Picture Library: pp. 5 (B), 76 (BR), 77 (BM).

T – top; C – center; B – bottom; TL – top left; TM – top middle; TR – top right; ML – middle left; MC – middle center; MR – middle right; BL – bottom left; BM – bottom middle; BR – bottom right.

*Jaguar car on page 21: Courtesy of **Corgi Toys Ltd** (a Mattel company)*
*Illustrations on pages 7, 9 and 89: **Stefan Chabluk***